Alexander's Path

Alexander's Path

A Travel Memoir By
Freya Stark

THE OVERLOOK PRESS
WOODSTOCK, NEW YORK

First published in 1988 by
The Overlook Press
Lewis Hollow Road
Woodstock, New York 12498

Library of Congress Cataloging-in-Publication Data

Stark, Freya.
Alexander's Path : from Caria to Cilicia / Freya Stark.
p. cm.
Reprint. Originally published: London: J. Murray, 1958
Bibliography: p.
Includes index.

1. Cilicia—Description and travel. 2. Pamphylia (Turkey)—
Description and travel. 3. Lycia—Description and travel.
4. Alexander, the Great, 356-323 B.C.—Journeys—Turkey.
5. Arrian. Anabasis. 6. Turkey—Description and travel—
1960-   7. Stark, Freya—Journeys—Turkey. I. Title.

DS165.S74   1988   913.9'2—DC19   87-34554
ISBN: 0-87951-309-8

To B.B.,
whose kind thoughts travelled with me,
this book is dedicated.

My grateful thanks are due to Lord David Cecil, to Sir Harry Luke, to Dr. Guy Griffith, to Mr. John Sparrow, to Mr. George Bean; to the Editor of *The Journal of Hellenic Studies* for permission to reprint the article which appears as Appendix I, and to my patient publisher for kind advice and help.

'He lived thirty-two years and eight months ... In body he was very handsome, a great lover of hardships; of much shrewdness, most courageous, most zealous for honour and danger, and most careful of religion; most temperate in bodily pleasure, but as for pleasures of the mind, insatiable of glory alone; most brilliant to seize on the right course of action, even where all was obscure; and where all was clear, most happy in his conjectures of likelihood; most masterly in marshalling an army, arming and equipping it; and in uplifting his soldiers' spirits and filling them with good hopes, and brushing away anything fearful in dangers by his own want of fear—in all this most noble. And all that had to be done in uncertainty he did with the utmost daring; he was most skilled in swift anticipation and gripping of his enemy before anyone had time to fear the event; he was most reliable in keeping promises or agreement; most guarded in not being trapped by the fraudulent; very sparing of money for his own pleasure, but most generous in benefits of others.

'If Alexander committed any error through haste or in anger, or if he went some distance in the direction of Eastern arrogance, this I do not regard as important; if readers will consider in a spirit of charity Alexander's youth, his unbroken success, and those courtiers who associate with kings ... But I do know that to Alexander alone of the kings of old did repentance for his faults come, by reason of his noble nature....

'Whosoever speaks evil of Alexander ... let such a one, I say, consider of whom he speaks evil; himself being more puny, and busied about puny things, and not even bringing these to success.'

ARRIAN VII, 28–30.

CONTENTS

*

FOREWORD   XV

PART I

CILICIA

1. ISSUS AND CASTABALA   3
2. MERSIN, SOLI AND OLBA   13
3. CILICIAN DIGRESSION.   *Seleuceia to Anamur*   25
4. CILICIAN DIGRESSION.   *Anamur to Antalya*   41

PART II

PAMPHYLIA

5. THE PAMPHYLIAN PLAIN   57
6. MOUNT CLIMAX   73
7. THE PAMPHYLIAN DEFILES   89
8. SELGE   104

PART III

LYCIA

9. THE CHELIDONIAN CROSSING   121
10. THE VALLEY OF THE ALAǦIR CHAY   131
11. THE EASTERN WALL OF XANTHUS   146

Contents

12. THE COAST ROAD OF LYCIA   160

13. THE ROAD TO FINIKE FROM MYRA   174

14. THE HIGHLANDS OF XANTHUS   185

15. OENOANDA AND THE PASSES OF XANTHUS   196

16. THE WALL OF XANTHUS   212

APPENDIX 1 (with maps):

    ALEXANDER'S MARCH FROM MILETUS TO
      PHRYGIA   229

APPENDIX 2:

    APPROXIMATE MILEAGES   257

REFERENCES   259

BIBLIOGRAPHY   269

MAP   272

INDEX   273

FOREWORD

*All the business of war, and indeed all the business of life, is to find out what
you don't know by what you do; that's what I called 'guessing what was at the
other side of the hill'.*

DUKE OF WELLINGTON: *Croker Papers,* 1885, Vol. III, p. 276.

NO PART OF THE WORLD CAN BE MORE BEAUTIFUL THAN
the western and southern coasts of Turkey. Their
remote valleys break from the treeless plateau, whose
oozing snows feed them with harvests wherever the land is
flat enough to grow wheat or barley; and to travel in and out of
them is like the circumventing of an immense natural fortress,
whose walls are precipices with a glacis of fertile stretches
before them and whose bastions are toilsome capes that dip,
one after another, to the sea.

I have made three journeys into these regions, and have
written two books about them—the first dealing with the more
northerly and gentler coasts of Ionia, and early blossoming of
Greece on the easy peninsulas loved by the Mycenean oarsmen;
and the second travelling by sea, under the high, forest-clad
fortresses of Lycia. When I left these, I longed to return, and
after a two-year interval did so, and my account now extends
the scope of the former journeys, describing things that already
have altered much since I saw them, round the coasts and
along the southern shore from Alexandretta to Pamphylia,
into the valleys of Chelidonia and the uplands of Cibyritis
behind them. The method of travel, by horse or jeep along
ways not much frequented, brought me into closer contact
than before with the country people of Turkey, whose kindness,

hospitality, and goodness I am delighted to have discovered for myself, as many earlier travellers have done before me.

This, then, was a simple travel book to plan. Beginning at the beginning it was to move, like the voyage itself, by easy human stages to its end; and so it would have done, if Alexander, and the geography of his marches, had not pressed in to complicate the pattern.

Alexander followed this coast and crossed the Chelidonian headland, and although that early and successful adventure is dismissed in few words by all historians ancient or modern, the mere outline of the great conqueror's footstep is enough to oust all other history from one's path. He impressed himself upon me not all at once, but gradually, as the descriptions of Arrian and the scenes of the landscape combined; and I have kept this accidental order, and brought him by slow degrees into my story—stepping into the foreground at Issus and vanishing altogether through Cilicia, along the pirate coast. It was only when I first reached Pamphylia in 1954, that a question—like that small discrepancy which starts the train in detective stories—awakened a number of surmises. I was driving along the plain, dark under the sunset, with pointed ranges round it thin like cut paper against the clear pale sky. Looking, as Alexander must have looked, at the easy spaces on my right that seemed to lead to open valleys, and at the opposite heavy high outlines of Termessus threatening in the west: " why," I asked myself, "should he have wished to turn west at all and attack such a difficult position, when his aim was all towards Gordium in the north?"

This question altered what was left of my journey. Instead of adding the Macedonian march down the coast to my Lycian book, as I had intended, I held my hand and decided to investigate the passes and to see whether Arrian had not left out things that it might still be possible to discover. The whole route between Xanthus and Phaselis, and the campaign against the hillmen which it included, is a blank, to which roads and passes are, I felt sure, the key. I began to ask myself other questions. Why, if they had no importance, should Arrian mention those mountain raids from Xanthus and Phaselis? And why, if one comes to that, should Alexander stop here and there for unessential reasons while his greatest adversary was gathering in strength before him? It seemed as improbable as did the unnecessary turning to the west. Only one other mountain raid is mentioned before Issus, and that too dealt with passes—near Soli in Cilicia—evidently intended to secure the road to the coast from Labranda (Karaman). I decided to spend two months with a horse or a jeep among these mountains, and reconstruct what I could.

*   *   *   *

It is one of the caprices of history that while the farther regions of Alexander's marches have been illuminated by the most brilliant modern scholars and enquirers, the nearer geography of Anatolia, which saw the first and most formative year and a half, or perhaps a little more, of his adventure, have been comparatively little attended to. The ancient historians dismiss it in a few pages, and the moderns are not left with much to work on; and this is perhaps due to the fact that Asia Minor, now full of elusive distance, was a part of the everyday world in Alexander's time. The crossing of the Hellespont was a military risk and an imposing function, but no leap to the unknown. Alexander must have been familiar with it through Aristotle, who had spent three years and married at the philosophic court of the tyrant of Adramyttium, and had then lived in Mitylene. His host, the uncle of his wife, met ruin and death through the Persians' governor, Memnon the Greek—which adds a private enmity to the first campaigns in Asia. Among the most intimate of Alexander's friends and companions were the Lycian Aristander and the Cretan Nearchus, who knew the coastlands well; and there had been messages and intercourse with Caria, and friendship in Philip's court with Persian refugees.

There was no need to go into great detail of routes in a country so well known; and the king who landed here was not yet solitary in his Arimazian mists, but a companion whose projects were shared by all his peers. It is this little band of brothers, so very young, that swings across the Granicus, and looks out from the acropolis of Sardis, and takes Miletus and Halicarnassus by siege and storm and marches down the coast. Nor is there any mystery about their plans: they were those of a small army in a land where even Greeks were potentially hostile; the enmity of Athens was simmering, and no fleet but hers could stand up to the Persian navies at sea. The march through Caria, Lycia and Pamphylia was a measure directed not against the land forces of Darius, but against his ships. Alexander's objectives were the harbours with their populations of sailors and the immense forests behind them of cedar and cypress and pine, which continued through Hellenistic, Roman, Crusading ages to be valued and fought over by the timberless dynasties of Asia. When he reached Pamphylia, Alexander had in his possession all the harbours except the outlying fortresses in Caria which the Persians could hold from the sea; and when the battle of Issus was fought and won, he swung south and completed this naval policy along the Phoenician coast. Only then, with Tyre destroyed and Egypt conquered, was he able with no threat behind him to turn against the homelands of Darius.

When this policy was determined we do not know, but it was given a voice and an effect at Miletus, both during the siege and when Alexander disbanded the small navy he had.[1] From here he marched across Caria and besieged Halicarnassus and—leaving three thousand men to complete its capture behind him—continued down the coast. He knew all he had to expect in the rough hills of Lycia and travelled light, without siege train, heavy baggage, and possibly with little or no cavalry to speak of (which explains his anxiety about the horses of Aspendus when he reached riding country again). He foresaw no major opposition, for much of the infantry was left behind as well. He cannot have taken more than, or even as many as, fifteen thousand men.

Historians seem to me to have by-passed a certain human interest in this march, connected with Caria and Ada the Queen. The tangle of her affairs, complicated by incest and family quarrels, had ousted her from her throne and reduced her to the one fortress of Alinda. From here, Arrian tells us, she went to meet Alexander, surrendered her stronghold, and adopted him as her son. 'Alexander gave Alinda back to her in charge, and did not reject the adoptive title, and on the capture of Halicarnassus and the rest of Caria, put her in command of the whole.' Arrian does not even say that he stayed in her fortress—a fact proved by Plutarch, who mentions sweetmeats that she sent him every day, and how she offered to provide cooks—a picture of eastern hospitality and the difficulty of circumventing it which every oriental traveller will recognize across the ages.

Alexander therefore stayed in Alinda on his way, and became Queen Ada's adopted son; and all this began three years before, when he was still the nineteen-year-old prince in Macedonia, and had decided to marry Ada's niece. He had consulted the friends who were now among his officers, and had sent a messenger from Corinth to Asia. Philip, furious with him and with the companions who encouraged so inferior an alliance, had exiled a number of his friends. And now Philip was dead and the Carian family affairs had changed: Ada's brother, the father of the young fiancée, had ejected the widowed queen and become ruler; and he too had died, and Orontobates, a Persian brother-in-law, had seized and held his power. Ada, with all her difficulties, had become a centre for the anti-Persians in Caria. She would remember Alexander with kindness, and welcome someone who had almost become a member of her (however unsatisfactory) family: and that, it seems to me, is the background for the adoptive relationship of mother and son.

Nor is this matter historically negligible, though one would not wish to press it too far. Professor Tarn[3] has shown how important in the world's history were the thoughts of Alexander when they bridged the gap between Greek and Barbarian—the gap that Isocrates and Aristotle and every mainland Greek before him had failed to cross. Alexander crossed it. His messages from the Granicus speak of 'the spoils of the barbarians of Asia'; but tolerance grew as he came to know the lands and their peoples, step by step till it reached the climax of his life, and an unsurpassed conclusion; for at the feast in Opis, he prays for the brotherhood of mankind. And I do not think it too far-fetched to see in the planned half-Carian, half-Persian marriage in Asia—the boy's dream that prepared the reception of Alinda—an early step in line with the stronger steps that followed—the kindness for Sisygambis, mother of Darius, the marriage with Roxana, the Persian fusion, the gradual vision of a united world.

Any evidence of the links that unite this ancient dream, across a gap of twenty-two centuries, with our thoughts today, must interest us deeply, and give as it were a topical complexion to such events in Alexander's life.

The immediate effect, however, was that he passed through and out of Caria with influential friends. He came, too, as a champion of the democratic nationalists who were popular among the seafaring populations of the coast. Arrian, without lingering over names or details, brings him to Xanthus, mentions an expedition there among the tribesmen, brings him across the high peninsula to Phaselis and to Pamphylia, and finally takes him, after a fight in the defile of Termessus, north to Gordium where his base and his reinforcements and his general, Parmenion, were waiting. From there he marched by the regular and usual route with all his army, across the Cilician gates to Issus and his destiny beyond.

To find out what he did between Xanthus and Sagalassus became my object; and the gathering of the evidence and gradual unwinding of the clues got involved in my daily gossip of travel. I soon discovered that my book was no longer so easy to plan. Alexander and I happened to be travelling in opposite directions; he was coming from the north while I was approaching Chelidonia from the south. I could not very well treat myself like a movie roll and drive backwards along the southern coasts; nor could I reverse one of the most inspired marches in history. The only answer was separation. Alexander's progress is written by itself in the appendix to this book, with such evidence as to his route and motives as I have been able, to the best of my ability and very tentatively, to gather; and my own journey is related in the casual way which I enjoy. The Macedonians were never far from my thoughts: the places I visited were nearly always the places where they, too, had halted: the questions I asked myself were those that dealt with *their* geography, silent for so many centuries: but the order of my journeying remains haphazard as it occurred and the landscape is the landscape of today, though the past appears through it, like the warp in the world's threadbare weaving.

Yet it is, in spite of all this, a geographic essay, of which Alexander himself might have approved. For he was, more than most men, geographically minded. As I travelled, I remembered the story familiar in the East, as I heard it many years ago from the Mirza who taught me Persian in a garden in Hamadan. It tells how they spoke in the King's hall of the wells of life in the Lands of Darkness, and the King asked where they lay; and none could tell him until Elias, a stripling at the court, stood up and spoke of the waters, white as milk and sweet as honey, that rise through six hundred and sixty springs out of the darknesses of the west. Whoever washes there and drinks will never die.

Alexander, who wished to live for ever because his kingdom was so great, prepared for the journey. He asked what he should ride and Khizr Elias bade him mount a virgin mare, for their eyes are made of light—"and in truth," said the Mirza, "I have noticed that a mare which has never foaled sees better than any other—and each took in his hand a salted fish, to test the waters when they reached them.

"Now when they came to the western darkness, Elias wore a jewel, and by its glitter saw on every side white wells of water, and threw his salt fish, and it swam away; and Elias washed and drank and lives for ever. But Alexander of the Two Horns missed the path and wandered, until he came out by another road, and died in his day like other mortal men. Unto God we return."

The tale, in the way legends have, holds its essential truth and gives in right proportion the great conqueror's passion for exploration. I can even imagine, though there is nothing to prove it, that the secret promise of Ammon was no military matter, but the sailing of unvisited and unreported seas, for which on the shore of the Indian Ocean, 'he sacrified other sacrifices, to other gods, with different ceremonial . . . in accordance with the oracle given',[2] and reached perhaps the nearest limit of his dreams.

None can know. But to the geographical bent of Alexander's mind there is abundant witness, and the surveying section of his armies, checked and controlled by himself, long provided all the geography of Asia that there was. When his troops forced him to turn back he wept, not for the unfinished conquest—for he gave away the provinces of India as he acquired them—but for the unsolved problem with which his mind was busy when he died.[3]

Foreword

He was, one may venture to surmise, more of an explorer than an administrator by nature. His administration, at all events, was never proved, for he died too soon; but the ideas and innovations that underlay it can be traced in a normal way from clear beginnings, from Philip, Isocrates, Aristotle, Xenophon (whose contribution has, I think, been undervalued).[4] Distinct novelties, such as the acceptance of divine honours, which had already been given to Lysander,[5] the establishment of financial overseers, which Xenophon had foreshadowed[4]—these materials were transformed by his genius, but they lay there ready to his hand: and in military matters also the principle of growth is apparent—from Sicily through Epaminondas to the reorganization of the Macedonian armies; from Xenophon's first use of reserves,[6] to Cyrus and Agesilaus with their lessons for cavalry in Asia: the climax is as it were gradual.

But the explorer's readiness for the unknown, the quality that vivifies human darkness, the finding of the Waters of Life, to this—whatever the old Mirza may say—he attained. Combined with military genius it allowed him to conquer the world, and to hold its imagination as long as histories are written, and one responds to it now as men answered to it in his time. As he vanishes across the Asiatic ranges—with his veterans growing older, and his friends and officers about him writing the matter-of-fact details that Arrian copied—the atmosphere of legendary youth surrounds him, the explorers' atmosphere of The Tempest, which also grew from geographic origins in a remote, enchanted world.

Alexander's Path

PART I

CILICIA

Deseritur Taurique nemus, Perseaque Tarsos,
Coryciumque patens exesis rupibus antrum,
Mallos, et extremae resonant navalibus Aegae.
                    LUCAN: *Pharsalia*, III, 225.

Next day at dawn he passed the Gates with his
full force and descended into Cilicia.
                    ARRIAN, I, 4, 4.

1

ISSUS AND CASTABALA

Darius, then, crossed the height by the Amanian Gates and marched towards Issus; and he slipped in unperceived behind Alexander.

ARRIAN II, 7, I.

... when the two armies were close, Alexander riding along his front bade them be good men and true, calling aloud the names, with all proper distinctions, not only of the commanders, but even squadron leaders and captains, as well as any of the mercenaries who were conspicuous for rank or for any deed of valour. ... Once within range, he and his suite ... took the river at the double, in order to confound the Persians by the swoop of their attack.

ARRIAN II, 10, 1-4.

IN APRIL 1954 I TOOK A SEAT IN AN ALEPPO CAR WITH TWO Arabs, two English and a Turk, and the rain caught us before we were well out among the beehive villages that have mounded themselves through the ages against the skyline. There would be something eccentric about an oriental journey that made no false start to begin with, and we were lucky, for our one Turkish passenger was a man of influence, his new suitcase was on the outside of the roof where it was getting wetter than ours, and he was able and willing to make our driver turn back to hunt for a tarpaulin among his friends.

The driver was an Aleppo man, 'Aleppo, out of Aleppo, out of Aleppo for generations', and dusted his car cheerfully in the rain while we waited; and we set off for the second time with the feeling that all was in order. The rain continued: the Greco-Roman arch that marks the Syrian frontier was easily passed; at the Turkish border, more conscientious or less weather-conscious, they made us unload and load up again in sheets of water; and the afternoon was late before we crossed the marshy plain of Amuk, and battleship hulls of mountain closed about us dark and green. The tumbling red streams of Amanus washed across our road. For a moment we saw the plain behind us, wide-flooded and beautiful, in which Darius had camped with his army: then down to where the ships of Iskenderun (Alexandretta), like a row of sentinels, were anchored in their roadstead along the crescent of the shore.

'It was a trading place, and many merchant ships were lying at anchor,' says Xenophon of the lost city of Myriandus, and the same description will do for Iskenderun, its descendant, where the yearly British ships alone have increased in the last century from about forty to eight hundred. Mr. Redman, our Consul there, entertained me kindly, and lent me his car for the battlefield of Issus, which has been located some twenty miles away to the north on the banks of the Deli Chay.

The rain had been just such a storm as kept Alexander's army in camp on the November day before the battle in 333 B.C. But for it, he would have marched across Amanus, and Darius would have been able to seize and hold the passes behind him, and the world's history might have taken another course. As it was, I reflected, the swollen rivers would now make the scenery more or less the same. The whole plan of the landscape appears easily, in fact, to the imagination, the plain opening long and narrow between the flat shore of the Issic bay and the steep Amanus ridges, whose defiles like funnels fan their torrents out towards the west.

The march of Darius had, perhaps unintentionally (for it was done by a matter of hours) cut off the invader's army. The Persian king had brought his forces across a northerly pass, probably the very anciently frequented one of Bahche;[1] and he had descended on the roadstead of Issus and massacred the Macedonian sick that had been left there. When the news was confirmed, Alexander, who had already reached the neighbourhood of Iskenderun, waited only to give the troops their dinner, and marched them back in darkness to seize the narrow passage by the sea.

Only a ruin is left now—the shapeless fragment of a gate called the pillar of Jonah, where the Armenians later on had their customs,[2] with a medieval fort above; but Xenophon describes the wall of an earlier time, and towers on either side of a mountain stream, and Cyrus asking the Spartan ships to help him there as he expected trouble. Alexander in his turn took no chances, and kept his men surrounded by outposts 'on the crags' from midnight to dawn.

The mound of Issus, or possibly Nicopolis if those two are not the same, shows here beyond the American road and the railway, against the bay and the Aegean horizon. It is still a mere three cables[3] from the sea's edge, so that the shore-line cannot have retreated much since Cyrus pitched his tents there beside his anchored fleet. The only city at that time was Issus; and the present half-way village of Payas, with its bridges, mosque, minaret and old castle, is not visibly earlier than the ages of Islam. Towards the open ground where it now stands Alexander descended in the first light, leading his troops in column. On the flat, he was able to deploy the phalanx, and brought up battalion after battalion to fill the space between the mountains and the sea. The cavalry, ranged behind the infantry, was brought forward, and the whole army —not more than twenty-nine thousand—marched on in order of battle, across what is now partly cultivation but then, being so thinly peopled, was probably scrub, easy and hard for the marching men to tread.

Descriptions of the battle mention the mountain, which pushes into spurs or withdraws in bays, so that the soldiers were crowded close at one time or spaced more thinly at another; and when the two armies came in sight of each other, the Persians raised their fierce confused war-cry, and the less numerous troops of Alexander heard their own voices enlarged and redoubled by the forest and the overhanging slopes. All this is very apparent as one crosses one after another the three parallel rivers that run their short impetuous courses to the shore. The Deli Chay has been identified with Pinarus, where the battle was fought; and I rather wondered why the more southerly Kuru Chay had not been chosen, giving as it does a ten- instead of a fifteen-mile march between the start at dawn and the opening of the battle, and crossing the plain at a slightly narrower place, more like the fourteen hundred stadia of Polybius. This measurement, I take it, refers to the narrowest section of the plain, which widens with every torrent that pours out of its defile in the range. This opening and shutting of the ground explains Darius' manœuvre. He stationed about twenty thousand men on the ridge 'that opened here and there to some depth and had, in fact, bays like the sea; and, bending outwards again, brought those posted on the heights to the rear of Alexander's right wing'. Centuries later, such manning of the heights of Issus gave a great victory to the emperor Severus;[4] but Alexander foresaw the danger, and as the plain widened brought forward the cavalry to the right wing where he commanded, and pushed patrols and archers to deal with the menace from the heights.

The three rivers looked very much alike, and I took the Deli Chay as the authorities offered it, and found it beyond the orange gardens of Dörtyol, or Fourways, flowing under the Ojakli bridge through a landscape of planes and poplars against the cloudy background of the hills. On either side of it the open ground sloped evenly and almost imperceptibly under beds of gravel that the floods of the ages have carried down. The pale rain-washed pebbles made easy banks, except where a bend, or a pressure of the current, scooped dwarf precipices, not high but crumbly: the sticks of the Persian stockade could easily be bent or pulled out from so yielding a foundation, which was nowhere too high for a man on horseback to be even with the defenders of the bank. The muddy current still looked as if it were tossing foam-crested manes of horses. The river had probably been lower, even after rain, in November, than now with the winter behind it.

I spent a long time here, imagining the battle very clearly, as Arrian and Curtius describe it, but puzzled by the flight. Alexander, safe across with the Persian left wing routed, turned to help his phalanx. It was in difficulties with the river-bank —which the horsemen had negotiated more easily—and with the Greek mercenaries who were charging for Darius from the top. Only when he saw the battle secure, did Alexander turn to pursue. This time it was evidently cultivated country, as one would expect in the neighbourhood of a city like Issus, for 'the riders were hurrying by narrow roads in a crowded horde . . . as much damaged being ridden over by one another as by their pursuers': they were no longer in the scrubby open where they could scatter.

Darius had seen his officers killed around him, with their faces on the ground as they had fallen, their bodies covering their wounds'. He fled in his chariot, as long as he found it level; and 'when he met defiles and other difficulties, left his chariot and threw away his shield and his outer mantle, nay, left even his bow in the chariot, and fled on horseback'; and these things were found by Alexander, before the falling darkness turned him from pursuit.

Out of all this information, it seemed clear to me that Darius—whatever pass he took in coming, and the Bahche is the obvious one for a man with an army—cannot have fled except by one of the shorter tracks that led across the Amanus up the river defiles close by. Otherwise, if he had made for the northern pass, he would first of all have met no defiles for hours, to force him on to a horse; his retreat would have led him near enough to his camp to pick up his family in passing; and lastly, the finding of his chariot so quickly by Alexander—

easy enough at the mouth of a defile where only one road is available—would have been much more of a coincidence on the wide northern plain. I looked longingly at the likely pass, which opens to steep high pastures east of Erzin, and can be ridden across in twelve hours, they told me, to the Amuk plain: but the snow still lay thick upon it, and would do so until towards the end of April; and I have not yet been across. The Consul's Greek driver took me back to Iskenderun, discussing tactics; and I left next day for Adana and Mersin, with four Turks and a Turkish colonel's wife in a car.

Castabala

On this, the second of my Turkish journeys, I still spoke very little of the language. I sat, usually in the 4th century B.C., but otherwise alone, while the tides of life rippled around me, and was roused from such torpor by the bulk of the colonel's wife pressing me into the middle of the front seat for which I had paid double to enjoy it by myself. The colonel and a friend were seeing her off, and they and the driver and all the passengers looked at me, when I protested, with that furniture-look which the old-fashioned Turk keeps for women who begin to make themselves conspicuous in public. I might have been a fly walking up a window-pane within their field of vision. The driver's conscience pressed him to say "zarar yok" (it doesn't matter) at intervals; but the woman continued to sit. The British lion disguised as a worm suddenly woke up inside me, and I vaulted over her thighs and wedged myself between her and the window, so that the colonel when next he turned round found that he was no longer talking to his wife. A horrid silence followed. The six men remonstrated; I fixed my eyes on a roof, and they gave it up. The colonel went off, looking absent-minded. Having obtained justice I was willing to be amiable. I explained how necessary the window-seat is to a photographer; and a thin little melting of friendliness trickled back into the car.

This was helpful, for no sooner were we out on the open road than two policemen broke from a mulberry hedge, held up their hands, and asked to see what was in my five pieces of luggage on the roof. Having been soaked to the skin to show them at the frontier two days before, I was naturally put out, but there was nothing to be done: unsuitable objects were spread out in the dust while the army, firmly holding its rifles, looked on.

"Can't *any* of them be bought in Turkey?" the sergeant asked, bewildered, appealing to the landscape where the battle of Issus was visible in the distance.

By this time an obliging engineer had climbed out from the back and advised that if I had some little scrap of paper given at the frontier, all would be well. I had, and handed it. It was what was wanted, and the fault was mine for not knowing all about it. The soldiers became filled with kindness. They tried in a pathetic way to help me pack. They had done their destruction with no malice—no official sadism—merely an anxiety to Do Right—an awful thing in Men of Action uninfluenced by Words! I spurned them, and worked on by myself moaning "zahme, zahme, sorrow, sorrow", as I did so: but when all was over, and the luggage tied on to the roof again, we were reconciled. It was their work and duty, said they. It was hard and disagreeable for them to have to do it, said I. We shook hands and parted and the engineer at the back expressed his enthusiasm over the army's condescension: "but it was your politeness," he added, "that won them over." I felt I had been British enough for one morning, and let it go, entranced by eagles which I afterwards heard were vultures, soaring over Issus in the sun.

A flat expanse wide as a plain, the Jihan or Pyramus valley, lay open before us, with the Iron or Amanic Gates of the

Cilician highway on its western edge.[5] They were not much
to look at: sloping like Victorian shoulders, one behind the
other they sank to nothing: but they were at the meeting of
great thoroughfares and people had come and gone here continuously, either by Alexander's route to Syria or by Bahche
eastward to Mesopotamia. A way led up from them through
an openness already green with summer, and an Arab castle
of basalt on a stepped mound stood guard. It was called
Toprak Kale and was the first I had seen in Turkey with that
fairy-tale completeness of the Islamic fortress. The walls and
towers went up diagonally across its grass-grown terraces, in
a shallow landscape of smooth green hills.

At the top of the trouée, some ten miles away beyond the
Pyramus (Jihan), the line of the pass is again held by Castabala
—now Bodrum. There, according to Curtius, Alexander
joined Parmenion, sent ahead from Tarsus to secure the passes.
This cannot be true, for Alexander marched by the coast, while
his cavalry moved straight eastward and joined him by the
Amanic Gates; and Arrian is explicit, and gives no time for a
detour and two river crossings to be added to a march of over
thirty-five miles in two days.[6]

But Curtius' source perhaps referred to Castabala territory,
which could easily stretch so far south: and Parmenion probably reached the northern fortress, for he patrolled the outlets
of all the passes with his Thessalian horse before joining Alexander in the march south to Issus.

Just after the Macedonians had gone, Darius came into this
valley and turned south down its natural avenue towards the
sea. The Bodrum fortress is a descendant of the one that
must have watched him, whose stones can still be seen in the
foundations. It is a small castle left on a rock by the Knights
of St. John, with towers slanting together like a handful of
spears. At its back the ridge was cut through in more ancient
days to make a passage of over fifteen feet between two halves of

a city. A street of columns with brackets and late Corinthian capitals led down from it in Roman and Byzantine ages, and half-fallen apses of buildings, Christian or pagan, stand deep in corn, as if all were ripening for the same harvest. A wide and glowing view basks in the sun. The northern track, still used, rises between tilled hillsides; on the north-east are the far 'pierced mountains' of the Arab wars; and the river in front fills its curves from bank to bank with a strong current, where the years can see themselves reflected as they ride by.

Darius found it not very different. The fire altars were carried across the pass and the young men in red cloaks marched before him; and those who led the chariot and the horses of the sun; and the twelve nations; and the Immortals with their apples, in sleeved tunics and gold; and the King's relatives that surrounded his high car; and the thirty thousand footmen and the four hundred horses; and the six hundred mules and three hundred camels with money; and the chariots of the mother and wife, the women and children behind: all this Curtius tells, as some Greek soldier must have seen it, who describes with professional disgust the 'discordant, undisciplined army' in the camp before Issus.

But we, driving through the Amanic Gates at the southern end of the great avenue on this particular day, saw nothing of all that, for we followed the main road of the plain. We passed under the Castle of Snakes, where the stubble was burning, and storks, like diplomats with narrow shoulders and well-tailored cut-away clothes, walked about without any signs of enjoyment, swallowing frogs that jumped from the flames. We passed Missis, the ancient Mopsuestia, a shabby little town of decay, whose bridge was built by Valerian and repaired by Justinian, and Walid and Mu'tasim,[7] when the Pyramus was one of the rivers of Paradise and sailed by Tancred's galleys;[8] we ran through cotton fields, whose cultivation began with the Crusaders and was renewed by Muhammad Ali; and came to Adana, filled with noisy streets; and to Tarsus across the yellow Cydnus—not clear as it once was, but thick with mud, as if Time and all ruins were inside it—between banks where Alexander bathed and the Caliph Ma'mun died, and Julian the Apostate was buried. But as for us, we drove to Mersin and the friendliest of living welcomes at the Toros hotel.

2

MERSIN, SOLI AND OLBA

He took a guard into Soli, and fined them two hundred silver talents, because they were still inclined towards Persia . . . and marched upon the Cilicians who held the heights. In seven days—no more—he partly drove them out, partly received surrenders, and returned to Soli.

ARRIAN II, 5, 5–6.

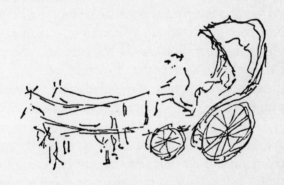

MERSIN, AS A RESORT, HAS LITTLE TO RECOMMEND IT. It is built along a flat beach, with no known history; and Captain Beaufort, charting this coast in 1812, found nothing but a few huts and some ancient tiles scattered on the malarial level. Prosperity began with the Crimean War and a demand for cereals,[1] and tobacco and cotton now ensure it; wooden piers and jetties are multiplying along the shallow sands; and streets and houses add themselves behind them. A club, a 'family garden', a casino and cinemas are there, and the market starts at 4 a.m. in summer with shoeblacks seated in a row, their boxes bright with brass ranged like portable altars before them. The box is not only useful to hold polishes and brushes; it is a symbol of the confraternity, and cannot be merely bought with money. From the window of my hotel I dropped my sandals down and watched them being treated with that artistic enthusiasm which the Middle East concentrates on its shoes, however shabby; and I could then lean out and look at the market unloading lorry-loads of vegetables, and see the level sun pushing shafts into dingy crannies, to give the illusion that even the flotsam of the man-made world still shares the life of nature.

A good traveller does not, I think, much mind the uninteresting places. He is there to be inside them, as a thread is inside the necklace it strings. The world, with unknown and unexpected variety, is a part of his own Leisure; and this living participation is, I think, what separates the traveller and the tourist, who remains separate, as if he were at a theatre, and not himself a part of whatever the show may be.

A certain amount of trouble is required before one can enter into such unity, since every country, and every society inside it, has developed its own ritual of living, as well as its own language. Some knowledge of both is essential, and—just as our circumambient air contains melody but cannot express it until a voice is given—so a technique or voice is needed for human, or indeed for all intercourse. To find this unity makes me happy: its discovery comes unexpectedly upon me, not only with people, but with animals, or trees or rocks, or days and nights in their mere progress. A sudden childish delight envelops me and the frontiers of myself disappear; I feel sorry for, but also try to avoid, the human beings who estrange themselves in separate cells like porcupines in needles.

In Mersin, neither language nor knowledge were sufficient. I was at home in the hotel, whose owner overflowed with kindness and with a passion for cleanliness unique in my experience of Turkish inns; but, when I went out to eat at the *lokanta* on the beach, a dusty little wind fretted the oleanders, and the waiter tried to talk French, and the feeling would come over me that They and I were different—the root of all troubles in the world.

As my meal was finished and people had left, I sat on, watching a woman in check trousers; she was holding a pail of tired vegetables and talking to a man who had married her daughter. "She is begging him not to gamble," the waiter came up and explained, unasked, in simplified language that I might understand. So one is drawn in. The son-in-law saw her off and returned—small, weak, curly-headed, with yellow shoes and showy pullover; not good nor bad, but boneless. He sat and ate at the expensive restaurant and wasted his beer half finished, and I wondered where his wife lived—in some dingy little hole. At the end of each meal time, when the people had thinned out, the mother-in-law took her pail of garbage and went off with a meagre white-haired man, who sat feeding his dog till she came. The dog too was a caricature. His hind leg was broken, and he limped with his masters—a trio held together by affection in a world that gives them little, and touching, because of the razor-edge we live on, to us all.

When I got back to the hotel another drama was being developed. A woman sat looking out to sea, dabbing her eyes and bursting into Arabic regardless of the public lounge. She was very fat, and obviously came from across the border, and another immensely fat woman soon joined her. How unjust, that tears should look ridiculous when one is fat! The one man in the party thought so too, and slunk out quietly when the new arrival released him, leaving the great harim background of Asia to operate alone.

Next morning I drove westward in a taxi across the plain that even in the days of Cyrus grew 'sesame, millet, panic, wheat and barley, and is surrounded on every side, from sea to sea, by a lofty and formidable range of mountains'.[2] It narrows, until the rough Cilicia closes the coast with snouts of limestone and the difficult haunts of the pirates begin; and the last of the ancient cities before it closes was Soli, whose proverbial loutishness gave our language the word *solecism*—a place now filled with orange gardens and prosperous small houses, that have planted their foundations on the line of its former walls. Out of the two hundred pillars of the colonnaded street which the Hellenistic age invented, twenty-three still stand; a heaped mound near-by shows the theatre; and an artificial oval harbour, built with moles to protect it, is filled with a petrified beach where the sea washes shallow, as if over a concrete floor. Peasant women had come down to picnic; their young girls were flying kites from the headland; their horse was tethered beside its cart; and along the shore the dunes stood in column to hold the sea-wind back. Alexander fined the city for its Persian leanings, and stayed to review his forces, and held his games here: and during this stay, marched away for a week to deal with the country of the hillmen.

He had to safeguard the only good alternative route west of the Cilician Gates. It leads from Corycus and Silifke and the Gök Su valley—the ancient Calycadnus—to Karaman and so to the plateau south of Konia,[3] and is possibly the route by which Epyaxa the Queen of Cilicia was sent to the coast by Cyrus.[4] On its south-eastern edge was the priest-state of Olba, whose temple, built some time about the year 300 B.C., stands with columns still upright at Uzunja Burj, the ancient Diocaesareia. It has been excavated and is accessible in summer to a car, twenty miles or so north-east of Silifke; and I drove there partly for the pleasure of seeing columns that have not been thrown down, and partly because it seemed to me that this centre of religion, influential in its district long before the age of Alexander and—as far as I could judge—not more than two days' march from Soli, was the most likely target for his week's campaign. The hillmen 'were partly driven out and partly sent in their surrender' and, some time after Alexander's death, his officer Seleucus—a handsome

16

young soldier whose head in bronze is in the Naples museum—succeeded to this country. He built or helped to rebuild the temple, and founded Seleuceia, now Silifke; and from his first visit probably remembered the importance of the strategic Calycadnus at its opening to the sea. He maintained friendly relations with Olba: and it was pleasant to follow these young footsteps, by the gorges that open like traps in the ramparts of Taurus, and clean bays and shallow headlands and sandy fringes of the pirate realm. The detail was permanent rock, such as the Greek genius knew round all its coasts; it lifted itself out of the sea-glitter to shine in spite of harshness, like the Greek civilization itself on the radiant shores.

I had hoped to ride up by the Lamas, but floods were pouring through the gorge to the level of a man's shoulder, and we crossed a camel-backed bridge crowded among willows and drove on. Bulldozers were building the wider road and a new bridge may now scarcely notice the historic little river, the armistice line between Saracens and Crusaders where prisoners were exchanged during the Arab wars.[5] Pompey, when he defeated the pirates, settled many of them as citizens in Soli, and the whole of this coast turned gradually into a string of seaside suburbs, easy and secure in Roman times. All has fallen, but the suburban atmosphere remains. As I drove during this day, I counted over fifty shafts of marble column, in pieces or entire, and all doomed; some lay in the ditches, or pushed half out of banks where the road was cutting, or made dykes for irrigation, laid end to end. And the ruins of a whole world were scattered at the roadside, in tombs, or the double aqueduct of Sebaste that strides for six miles across ravines and gullies, or Sebaste itself on its rise, or the castle of Elaeussa and the older Byzantine castle on the island, that with all this coast except Seleuceia had been given by Antony to Cleopatra; or the apses of Corycus churches, crowned with thorns.

The fertile lands at the mountain feet grow narrower by the

Lamas river, and we now ran along an older road, with never a car but horses and goats at its corners, close in to the curve of the sea that lay in morning peace as if chiselled, as if the joy of life were hidden there in metal. From beyond the horizon one felt the invisible light, as if a Siren were singing; and the strange electric water held white capes whose undercut edges gave them a rim, like eyes dark with mascara. A porpoise was turning over and over in the bay.

"How wonderful, how exquisite to be alone," he seemed to say.

The two castles faced each other, with stones of a mole between them whose buildings have vanished; where a brook coils its small estuary in marshy mirrors to the sea.

At Corycus, a paved way leads to where the hollow hill has slipped into a cavity, a Plutonium in whose depths Picrum Hydor, the Bitter River, is heard.

"Do the waters flood to the surface?" I asked an old peasant who took me.

"No," said he. "They would," he added, "if the Government installed a pump."

Five arches of a Byzantine chapel are there in perpetual shadow, and saffron used to be found. It was exported in the early Middle Ages to make gold lettering for painters,[6] but modern travellers have not seen it. Half a dozen or so have written about this region—Olivier in the 18th century, Leake, Beaufort, Davis, Kinnear, Bent, Heberdey and Wilhelm; and Michael and Mary Gough, who were kind to me with advice, have made the present Cilician coast their own. The road is still new, and not many have been along it. Its civilized feeling, its tombs and aqueducts and earth so stuffed with columns, came in the train of Alexander, who found the land more solitary even than now, and the ancient worship alone among its hills. The Greece of Macedonia produced this clutter of Roman ruins; and Theodoret, many years later, talking to a hermit in North Syria, was surprised to find that he spoke Greek because he came from Cilicia.[7] The world's hellenizing was the young men's achievement; and sometimes, waiting for a train on the London District Railway, I have looked at Corinthian capitals, cast in iron, that hold the stations up, and have thought how they too came to us through the march of Alexander and his companions into Asia, in 334 B.C.

The people of the Middle East (who are the only people beyond Europe that I know) think that an external discipline is sufficient to reproduce a way of life which they admire, and which strangely enough happens to be ours. Now this is not a thing that can be handed over or imitated. It cannot be done. No living organism can be copied; for a civilization is not made by mere acts, but by the traditions and impulses behind them. These alone can be handed on, to be assimilated, nurtured, and reborn in a new shape, alive and different in new hands. Unless such a process takes place the mere imitation is dead.

The invaders of the Greek and Roman world too copied, and we call their labour decadence, and wonder at the chasm that divides it from its lovely inspiration. Their clumsy efforts were mere effigies; the true descent was evolved slowly from some assimilation that fashioned it in centuries of Seljuk or Byzantine, or in far Norman cathedrals that have lost even the memory of whence they came. Because this hidden process is so sorrowful, we rightly hesitate to press our western pattern, or try to plait it in sparingly, so as not to destroy other strands which may be good. Nor do we feel sure that what we offer is better than what the imitators lose.

This feeling is dimly at the root of what the Arab and other nations continue to think of as a grudging attitude towards their own modernity. They prevent us, if they can, from taking even a picture of their old world; nor will they believe that their own tradition already possesses what anything copied from aliens can only acquire by a long process of adoption and change. A doubt has come upon us, whether what we offer is really worth such sacrifice; and it is this sentiment, the very opposite of envy, which makes any civilized westerner regret any country's absolute denial of its past.

No such uncertainty was felt, or required to be felt, by Alexander and his armies; and the way of life they planted has endured. Like an underground river, like the Corycian waters, it tunnels through hollow places, and wells out in new soil—Indian or Arab or English, Western or Atlantic or Asian—binding all with that invisible thread which was once the Greco-Roman world. What it failed to reach has mostly remained barbarous even today, and for my part I have no wish ever to live beyond its decent orbit.

We now turned from the coast and its echoes to where the seaside towns went in summer under the Roman peace. A road opens from the valley of the Calycadnus when Seleuceia is in sight, and soon turns eastward, with a merciless surface, and slabs of an ancient highway here and there. At its edge, like some via Appia more widely scattered, the tombs continue—sometimes a plain sarcophagus, or a temple-chapel with a medallion in its pediment, the portrait of the dead. The summer-cities lay scattered not far to right and left, but hardly to be seen, so much had their walls and towers become coloured like the rocks. The nomads too, who inhabit all this country, begin now to settle and build houses, and naturally use old stones or perhaps build up an empty tomb. The gradually sloping land had once been honeycombed with settlements, especially where defiles begin to gnaw themselves down to the shore; but as we drove, those narrow places were out of sight below us; the undulating, rocky plateau, gently tilted three thousand and eight hundred feet above sea-level, hid the Aegean horizon and its troubles, the threats of invasion or pirates. There was no beauty, but a great delight in the pine-scented air. Oak trees began; woods filled the shallow depressions; the slopes were dovetailed to look like the folding of innumerable hands. A more inland country presently opened its cornfields; and, scrambling up to a solitary funeral tower, we saw the temple of Zeus-Olbius across an open valley, full in sight.

How beautiful these Cilician cities were—the marble street of Soli with Taurus behind it as you sailed to its oval harbour; and this on the sunlit hill! The columns are fluted half-way, the lower half-smooth, and all except four are broken off below the capital; the colonnade in the market near-by has the ugly fashion of brackets; and the triple gate that lets into it is late: there is no classic purity, but a comfortable feeling of tradition settled into life, and an intimacy, like that of an Oxford quad, in the shadows of the temenos under its almond trees. The theatre has fallen to ruin even in these hundred years, but the 1st century B.C. columns of Tyche, their five capitals intact under an architrave, stand clear as crystal against the revolving darkness of the sky. For the rest, there is only one heroic building in Diocaesareia, and that is a square Hellenistic tower of smooth and beautiful yellow stone on the outskirts of the village among cornfields. As on the pine-scented plateau, there was delight in the air of the temple, but of a sedate and bourgeois kind; the frieze gave it, carved with wild boars and dogs and oxen wreathed in leaves; and the wild roses that blossom against the columns give it too. Nor did its day-to-day pleasantness seem insufficient: for why should we need the heroic age in every ruin? Some day, in two thousand years or so, our descendants may rediscover the Houses of Parliament and decide that they belonged to a bad period; yet the life they sheltered had its good moments too.

Uzunja Burj is still inhabited. A school has been built, and the people of the coast come in summer to live three months or more in huts of twigs and leaves. The Democratic Party

Government has added a new water supply as its own contribution to history, and the neat cement in the valley takes the place of the well with its stone platform where generations of women have talked as they filled their goatskins. They were out now, doing the best they could with the municipal improvement by washing their clothes in it with unhygienic pleasure, while their cows drank at its source. The road led past them to Karaman between the teeth of small ridges, under oak trees not bright like ours, but dewy and dark as dreams.

The traveller, as he drew near the city, was met here by the population of its dead. Their Christian tombs without beauty crowd the low and steep façades of the narrow valley, which they restlessly puncture with holes: and the colonnades and Roman gate appear on the skyline beyond them, alive and desirable even now and a goal of journeys, a City on a Hill.

Olba itself, now called Ura, the priestly centre, is two or three miles away in the opposite direction, in a small enclosed plain where red earth full of stones was being tilled with wooden ploughs. A sacred way, 10.40 m. wide, and very steep, leads down to it between fallen columns worn to boulders; and there is now no village, but only a shepherd's hut or two patched up round Roman doorposts where the head of the defile drops and steepens. So sternly surrounded, the city, in spite of the oxen and the stubborn men behind them pushing their ploughs, looks as if some incantation had turned it back into the stone from which it came. Its garlanded tomb, and Severus' nymphaeum with steps and altars seem out of place under the hillside graves and climbing towers and aqueduct arches naked among the rocks. The priests and people, who had learnt how to live easy lives at Seleuceia, no doubt preferred, as anybody would, the fine air and open views of Diocaesareia, and saw with pleasure the colonnades of Alexander's successors civilizing their landscape, and welcomed the easy months of the year when carts and families and belongings trundled up from the heat of the coast.

With almost as much jolting as theirs we returned to the valley, crossed the Calycadnus where Barbarossa was drowned, and found a lodging in Silifke.   It is a busy prosperous market town, under a Hospitaller castle with slightly waisted towers, and perhaps the compactness of castle and town and road and river, belonging so closely to each other, gives it a medieval rather than an ancient look.

A long bridge reaches it over six Turkish arches, slightly pointed. The stones that Vespasian, Titus and Domitian put there are probably still inside it; and[8] this bridge, narrow and paved, with parapets one higher than the other decorated with stone knobs like turbans, polished by centuries of weather— this long bridge, visible from all the river-houses, is the key to the existence of Silifke, at the meeting of the northern and the coast roads, and the necessary crossing of the stream. It is still mostly horsemen who ride by, their busts only showing above the parapet, towards the town or the peaks of Anamur that stand like beds of hyacinths far away in the sunset. The castle with fine towers and wrecked interior looks down from its hill on minarets and market streets, trees and the end of the cultivation. It is inseparable and, like a stone in its setting, is isolated from all except the river and the road. This medieval constraint, this small completeness, divides Silifke, in spite of its founder and its name, by many centuries from the sea-gaze of Greece.

As to my inn, too much space in travel books is, I think, devoted to the general slavery of life on journeys—so I shall dismiss it with the mention of a pretty wooden painted and arcaded court, up very dusty stairs. Here, surrounded by dilapidation, I found a room to myself (always a difficulty); and having had someone's ash-tray cleared away, a clean jug of water brought, the sheet and quilt changed for safety and the window (pasted down with paper) cut open, felt that the night was not so hopeless after all. There was little to be done about washing, at a sink of grey stone with two taps in the open; and the sanitation in these small places is no pleasure: but that was the worst. The day had been long—fifteen hours in a car or walking—and as I had now learned how to manage the cotton quilt so as to lie inside it in comfort, as if it were a cocoon, I was very soon asleep.

3

CILICIAN DIGRESSION

Seleuceia to Anamur

From this haven in former times has come forth a powerful army of pyrats with 1000 sayle, so proudly rigged, as many of them had their sayles of purple, the tackling of golden thread, and the oars garnished with silver; marks of the spoyle of above four hundred cities ruined . . .

Grimstone's *General History of the Turks*: by Knolles, Lond.; 1638, p. 1328.

THE CASTLE OF SILIFKE WAS CLOSE ABOVE THE TOWN WITH apparently no approach at all. An Italian municipality would have given it a 'panoramic drive' and spoilt it in the process, but the Turks, in a land more encrusted than any other with history, are almost unbelievably uninterested in ruins. The castle hillside is empty, except for a strange arcaded Roman reservoir dropped into a hollow, and a few bare tombs. A cloth merchant from his shop took me, and sang patriotic songs at the top, proud to have negotiated the shaly slope and to be, he told me, in possession of all his teeth at forty-six. This question of teeth was always brought forward during a village conversation, and I gained credit for having kept mine beyond the usual span. But it was a poor subject to contemplate from the heights of the Calycadnus. The merchant's cousin was more congenial, and pointed out the winding river and inland road the lorries take, that return to the coast through Gulnar. The sea road was new, cut only three years before and still presumably unknown to the foreign world, for my friends in Smyrna, Cyprus and Syria had denied it. Kinnear had ridden there along a path two feet wide, a century ago;

25   D

but a pre-Roman way once existed, and traces of a stony track remain, slipping unobtrusively at intervals beside the new road, under the pines.

A wind came rushing down the Calycadnus in the night, burst open a window in spite of the paper pasting, furbished the stars and moon, and ushered in one of those sparkling mornings with which the Cilician weather teases between its heavy storms. There was a cold brilliance, as if everything were beginning. A wayside mosque delayed us. Its columns had a capital both top and bottom, taken from classic Seleuceia on our right. That we left because the day was long before us. We drove past the Iskele pier by prosperous houses; across a river from whose stone-faced bank an ancient bridge must have been washed away—into the forest-clad solitudes.

All, on this and the next day's journey, was in the land of the pirates.

Apart from his dash up from Soli, Alexander left it alone. Looming out of its legends—Herodotus' Cilix the Phoenician, or Strabo's Cillus charioteer of Pelops, or Chilakka of the Assyrians,[1] it gathers destruction for later history like a cloud of its own mountains. In the Roman age the pirates hit the Levantine coasts. They ravaged Sicily and Ostia, and captured a consular fleet in harbour, and kept Romans off their own Appian way. They wasted bays and estuaries, 'till the seas were almost closed, and fleets dared not venture from Brundisium except in the depths of winter; and trade was at a standstill, and Rome itself threatened with famine'.[2]

Four hundred cities were said to have been sacked; coastal districts became barren and deserted; the slave markets of Delos could sell ten thousand human beings in a day.

The Athenians succeeded in keeping control, and so did Alexander; his admiral in 331 B.C. was given express command to clear the seas. His successors were apt to make allies of the pirates, but nevertheless they kept a certain authority: a papyrus of 248 B.C. shows that reserves of treasure and a Syrian governor could still be maintained in Cilicia. But when the Roman power defeated Antiochus the Great, and the peace of Magnesia was signed in 189 B.C., that king's navy was limited to ten warships, nor were they allowed to sail more than a few miles west of the Calycadnus;[3] and piracy revived. It was tolerated by the Romans, and together with the tax-gatherers provided slaves for a rapidly increasing demand. The miserable lands 'sought to avoid the ravages of the one by joining the ranks of the other'.

Men of intelligence and standing flocked to these lonely places, and became allies of warring kings like Mithridates. Ruined men came who knew the coasts and islands. They organized for war. The lighter boats were replaced by triremes that sailed under admirals in squadrons, and acted in concert. Cities like Phaselis, or Side in Pamphylia, flourished by providing markets and dockyards; and Crete defied Mark Antony's father, and bound the Roman captives themselves with the fetters they had brought.

Dio Cassius says that the Greeks suffered more from the Roman generals than from the corsairs, and Mark Antony's father was notoriously corrupt. After his failure, and the unappreciated victories of Lucullus, Pompey broke the last pirate strongholds on this coast. Seven hundred undamaged ships were collected for his triumph, one hundred and twenty castles were taken, and over twenty thousand pirates: they were shown not bound, but in their native costume; and the 'Syrian Fleet', in the early days of the Empire, was based on Seleuceia to watch this haunted sea. But Pompey, convinced that wretchedness and injustice alone had led the pirates to these excesses, settled them mercifully in the eastern Cilician plains— in places like Soli or Castabala, ravaged and depopulated through the Mithridatic wars, or in remote Achaia, or possibly in Calabria, with the old bee-keeper of the Georgics[4] from Corycus, where even now the bees are carried on camels every year to their summer pastures, to feed on thyme and myrtle in the hills.

Piracy revived with Byzantines, Crusaders, and Arabs who made it worse by using poisoned arrows; the seas again grew desolate and trade was forced inland: nor did the modern age stop it; for Newton writes in 1854 that 'last year Calymnos was suddenly invaded by a band . . . from Samos, about thirty in number . . . well armed. Choosing for the moment of their attack a time when the greater part of the male population was absent for the sponge fishery, they surprised and captured the lower town in open day, and sacked the houses and magazines of all the richest merchants'; and sailing from Rhodes to Finike—the sea that I feel I know—he describes a boat with four hundred on board attacked near Myra and the money taken. 'The same band, of seventeen, the day before attacked and sunk a small boat from . . . Symi and murdered the crew.'

Mr. Cockerell, about 1810, watched the pirate boats from Sunium, 'which is one of their favourite haunts'; and Captain Beaufort, in 1811, hunted such craft in his frigate, exactly off the shore where my taxi was driving into a deepening loneliness, a coastland of almost inaccessible peace.

The hills had run easily to sandy beaches till we approached the ancient Sarpedon, the six- or seven-hundred-foot-high Cape Cavaliere before which Agha Liman lay aslant in the sun, an octagonal fortress with two empty courts. They had been decorated in the 17th century by the pirates with the heads of forty Florentines, and a united nations expedition of that time rescued two hundred and forty other Christians within the walls and took six vessels and two warships from the bay.[5]

The ground was now sown with chickpeas in little ridges,

28

and a solitary dinghy lay stranded. Beyond the headland and a flat cape, good for the drawing up of boats, Provençal Island carried its ruins. No human being was in sight. I wandered along the battlements by narrow steps, and into three towers, and through the gateway that divides the courts, all roughly built. None of the polish, if there was any, had survived, but a naked memory of power remained. These alien castles spoke to each other from battlement to battlement, across forest and small tilled patches and hamlets with wattled chimneys, in unimportant undefended spaces: till their day passed and the land absorbed them, and they lie like stranded whales on its rocks and shores. When the Armenian king, Leo II, accepted Papal supremacy in 1196, he handed three of his Cilician fortresses to the Pope, who gave them to the Knights of St. John; and Agha Liman may have been one of them for all I know.

The country's spell began with the promontory. We climbed and saw pine-forests spread for hours of driving before us. They trooped in the sun over glossy ridges like droves of horses—their trees light and thin or dark and tall, according to the soil beneath them, or strewn park-like on patterns of their own shadows; and precipices of white or yellow or reddish limestone built a staircase of four thousand feet or more to the ribs of Taurus, that hid the Calycadnus and 'the long valleys of Cilicia'⁶ from our sight. The Mount Imbaros of Pliny—whose Cilician geography seems too untidy to deserve attention—has been identified as a ridge now called Sehler that travelled above us. Small beaches were wedged below, washed down between the high buttresses by winter streams; and where the rare bays opened, cottages, not poor but remote and simple—a door and two windows under a flat mud roof—would stand at the rise of the ground where the cornfields end.

The road lay loose as a string across headlands of broom and cistus. There one could watch ships bound to sail this side of the island of Cyprus, which soon appeared in sight; and the small pirate craft could put in to the almost unnoticeable wrinkles of the coast below. The same spell of peace probably held it then as now, in spite of its perils, for such sudden oases are one of the anomalies of danger. In 1945 when Italy was disturbed and occupied by the allied armies, I had occasion to drive with a friend down its western coast, by a similar empty slope, notorious at that time for bandits, and through the same sort of unnatural stillness. To the south of Viareggio, along the shore road, we noticed the extraordinary quiet of the pine-woods in the sun, and longed to find some little inn to lodge near the coolness of the sea. Some engagement next day luckily made me feel it necessary to push on in spite of the heat to Pisa, where we asked about the pine-woods, and found the subject rather noticeably dropped. It was only later, by accident, that I heard how a band of deserters of all nations had seized them, and filled them with arms, cars, guns, provisions, and women—the latter from Naples and the former from the American stores at Leghorn—and would almost certainly have shot at sight had we approached.

No such threats touch the coasts of Turkey, and nothing now disturbs their lonely safety. At the top of the precipice, above the cape, a castle stood high out of reach, with a round tower; and that was the last defence we saw for many hours. Our road sank to a few houses near the probable site of Holmi, Seleuceia's predecessor; it crossed a plain and river and mounted again. From its promontories we dipped in and out to pine-encircled hollows, filled with pomegranates, wild vines and laurel, or styrax with cup-petalled blossoms like white shadows, that grow over all this southern country in the woods.

The way was narrow, but we met no car, and only an occa-

sional rider, and high on the hillsides the goats enjoyed the
flatness and warmth of the road. They lay about it, their
herdsmen hidden, where paper-white cistus hung balconied
over the sea that stretched to Cyprus, misty and eyeless under
the sun.

In the rapture of such beauty,

'in the soft season
when the voice of Calm, the grey-blue daughter of Ocean,
quietly sings,'[7]

one could scarcely have borne a companion. One looked
not at but *through* experience, as if life in general were a window
to interpret the world, and this must be perhaps a solitary
pastime, the secret of travel. The stray roadside events are a
part of its solitude; but companionship—unless with one 'more
me than I am myself'[8]—produces the destructive shock which
every artist knows.

'Timon, when disturbed by maidservants or dogs, would stop
writing, his earnest desire being to maintain tranquillity.'[9]
Here, for hour after hour, tranquillity stretched from horizon
to horizon.

Before the afternoon, we reached an easier valley. A road
came down from Gulnar, and wild olives began to mix with
the carobs and pines. A poor and roughly built aqueduct ran
in a low wall to Celinderis—now Kilinderé—a colony said to
have been first founded by the son of Phaeton and then by the
people of Samos, and to be the oldest Greek site of the coast.
At the sea end of what was once an important road from
Karaman, and was still one of the two routes mentioned by
Leake in 1800, the ruined shabby little place clings to the edge
of a bay, 'a snug but very small port, from which the couriers
embark for Cyprus'[10] Even lately, an old man told me, the
Cypriots came across in boats to traffic, though all prosperity

is now half-buried under the rubble of British shelling in the first world war.

Apart from this, it is as Beaufort described it with its antiquities: an earthquake-rent tower, a small topless pyramid on arches, and vaults and tombs and fragments of mosaic, with one innovation—a pillar upside down in the little square—and a delicate pedestal of marble, a mare and foal in relief, fished out of the sea.

The change that has come over these coasts is in the people. In spite of his 'scrupulous anxiety not to offend their peevish prejudices', Captain Beaufort had trouble with many of his landings, whereas we sat among the elders with policemen from Istanbul. The Turkish Government has been intelligent and instead of urbanizing has made the village national; any student of the elementary school books can see how it is done. The stranger no longer drops as if from another world, but is received ceremonially by a community that feels it represents the nation, provided of course that their nation and yours are friends. Having made sure of this fundamental fact, they welcome you with a civility as strongly rooted as, though different in quality from, that of the Arab. The aloofness that asks no questions till food and rest have been provided is unknown: but the Turks look on a stranger as someone to be helped—and the added fact that women, however out of place, must not be left lying about makes a cosy restful atmosphere singularly Victorian, as one goes from place to place drinking their little glasses of tea.

A change had come over the landscape round Kilindere. It turned from limestone to shale, and broke its milky leviathan ridges to pointed contours and more hollow valleys. Fields of barley no longer overlapped the high flat summits, signalling inland villages safe out of sight of danger and the sea. The land between its rigid capes was mellowing into tillage. And where the more westerly route from Karaman ends near the

Philosophy of the Castle

Anamur plain, Softa Kalesi, an Armenian castle, suddenly revealed itself, a double wall round the top of a hill against a far snowy opening of Taurus.

My journey along this southern coast is a digression since Alexander never came near the country; and I do not want to make it worse by getting involved with the Armenians. But one must explain briefly that they came down from the Caucasus and produced a dynasty called the Rupenian,[11] from Rupin I in A.D. 1080 to Leo VI who lost his kingdom in 1375. They had spent the whole of the three centuries fighting Saracens, Byzantine emperors, Crusaders and each other, but chiefly Saracens; and though their main centres were in eastern Cilicia, they besieged Silifke too and seized this coastline, whose strongholds, until the Karamanlis and then the Ottomans took them, remained with intervals within their power. In A.D. 1199 they possessed a list of fifty-nine fortresses, and in the 15th century a Cypriot historian mentions two hundred forts and towns.

Perhaps, on a wide view, the medieval intrusion is not irrelevant after all. The mixture has made us, civilized barbarians of the north, and its harshness, rough but useful, is what Alexander too carried about within him, and showed in moments of emotion: then the Macedonian untutored language came back[12] in spite of his Hellenic training.

The importance of the castle is not in its trimmings of chivalry and later additions, but in the life which it protected, the hard, uninspired life tied down to necessity and labour, hidden in the long shadow of its walls. In most peasant countries there are roughly painted plates of earthenware that show the tasks of the twelve months—spring lambing and summer harvest, and the winter killing of pigs and cutting of timber. While the young men perhaps went off to fight with their pennants flying across the drawbridge, these were the realities which the castle sheltered and understood—hard country lives in which the sea, that had made Greece, counted little with its open horizons. The road was swallowed at either end in ignorance and twilight and rumour. And this life has given birth to countless civilizations, and buried them when they died. Such Alexander had in his mind when he spoke to his soldiers:

"... For Philip found you vagabonds and helpless, most of you clothed with sheepskins, pasturing a few sheep on the mountain sides, and fighting for these, with ill success, against Illyrians and Triballians, and the Thracians on your borders; Philip gave you cloaks to wear, in place of sheepskins, brought you down from the hills to the plains, made you doughty opponents of your neighbouring enemies, so that you trusted now not so much to the natural strength of your villages as to your own courage. Nay, he made you dwellers of cities, and civilized you with good laws and customs . . . opened up commerce to your country, and enabled you to work your mines in peace. Then he made you overlords of the Thracians, before whom you had long died of terror, and, humbling the Phocians, made the highroad into Greece broad and easy for you, whereas it had been narrow and difficult . . .

"All these noble deeds of my father towards you are great indeed, if looked at by themselves, and yet small, if compared with ours. I inherited from my father a few gold and silver cups, and not so much as sixty talents in his treasure; and of debts owed by Philip as much as five hundred talents, and yet having myself borrowed over and above these another eight hundred, I set forth from that country which hardly maintained you in comfort, and at once opened to you the strait of the Hellespont, though the Persians were then masters of the sea. . . . All goods things from Egypt and Cyrene, which I took without striking a blow, come to

34

you; the Syrian valley and Palestine and Mesopotamia are
your own possessions; Babylon is yours, Bactria, and Susa;
the wealth of Lydia, the treasures of Persia, the good things
of India, the outer ocean, all are yours; you are satraps, you
guards, you captains. . . ."[13]

This was the contrast in the mind of Alexander, which he
had to assimilate as we do—the sum of Hellene and barbarian,
which makes us what we are.

During the next few days, I climbed to Softa Kalesi, which
the Armenian historian identifies with Sig, Syce, or Sycae,
known as Sequin or Sequino to the Italians, and visited by the
French king in the 12th century when he passed along this
route to Anamur. It surrendered in the 15th century to
Joseph Barbaro, who gives an account of it, when Venice was
helping the Karamanli Sultan against the Ottoman Turks.[14]
If anyone wishes to go up to it, they can drive a Jeep from the
main road to Fidik Köy, and there find the only path up the
south side of the hill, and scramble to a square gate in the inner
wall (the outer gate has gone). A Gothic arch, with three
arrow slits west and one south, lets one in across courts and
buildings to the fort or keep, which has still preserved an upper
window and those triangle buttresses applied beside the door
which I believe are characteristically Armenian. Having
struggled round the two walls—the outer with round towers
and the inner with square—the visitor descending may drink
at the spring where the village leaves its gourds for any traveller
to dip with, and may perhaps explore the shapeless remnants
of the small ancient harbour of Arsinoe below; and then drive
west by a humped bridge over the Sini river (possibly Sikni,
which would suit the name of the castle), or Boz Yazi (the
names of the Anamur streams are desperately vague), through
Boz Yazi itself—a little centre of comfortable ramshackle
houses; and over the Kizilman cape to Anamur: and there the

plain will open out before him with such a view as no one in this everyday world can often expect to see.

A beach stretches in shallow loops to the southernmost cape of Turkey in the distance, eight miles or so away, with rich harvests sloping gently to the hills. There Anamur and its friendly villages are scattered, and another river, the Kara or Büyük Chay, the ancient Arymagdus, flows with poplars on its banks and flowering quinces, by an open valley from snowy passes that lead through Ermenek to Karaman. At the edge of the waves, crowned with towers on its flat shore as if time had never touched it, the castle of Anamur faces Cyprus, forty-five miles across the sea.

The place was called Staméné or Stalimore by the Crusaders, and Philip Augustus visited it on his way along the coast to Silifke; and the Venetians too brought sixty galleys and landed four hundred and forty knights with their squires, at the time when they took Softa Kalesi near-by.[15]

To all intents, it too is an Armenian castle, though a few older and better stones are visible at the foot of the south-west tower. In its later history, it was captured for the Karamanli Alaeddin whose inscription is over the west gate, and was lost in 1284 and recaptured. The Muslims repaired its battlements, built the mosque in one of its courts—bricked up now so that no browsing goats may defile it—and left the rooms of the inner keep with their pleasant Islamic comfort of living still apparent in decay. Peace pervades it now, all passion spent. The two long quads into which the interior is divided are there for meditation, with strips of shade under battlemented walls at all hours while the sun moves overhead. Narrow stone steps climb in diagonal parallels to the sentries' walk above, where I met a he-goat with wreathed horns browsing. Surprised as I was, he, after a moment's hesitation, sprang ten feet or more to the ground.

I spent six days here because I fell ill and was cured by a

doctor from Cyprus. His English, no better than my Turkish, filled me with the usual sorrow at our empire's past failures to teach those people it wished to keep inside. Partly too, I was delayed by the fact that my taxi could not be persuaded to go farther, and the single jeep of Anamur, devoted to the transport of registered letters, had to collect enough of them (or possibly only one) to make its journey worth while. The distances here are: one hundred miles from Silifke, one hundred and fifty-six from Mersin, and ninety to Alanya in the west.

The little centre itself, with a population of three thousand, in a district of twenty-three thousand altogether, was full of its own excitements. A general election was mounting to a climax of flags and lorry-loads of voters, and three newspaper reporters were there to ask what I thought of 20th-century civilization in Anamur. With so many ages to choose from, I felt I did not like whichever century the 'Banana Palas' hotel represented. A Caliban lurched in and out of my room without knocking, pouring water around me on the floor; and the proprietor, with a smile full of gold teeth and a rosary in his hand, appeared only to collect the rents which Caliban provided out of a ledger. A sick man coughed under his quilt all day in the general bedroom; and my own room, with four beds in it for all of which I paid (an extortion that never happened anywhere else in Turkey) was almost as expensive as the Ritz.

"It is not as comfortable as Mersin," I said to Nihat the driver; "nor was Silifke either."

"Well, no," said he, "of course not. Mersin is a little Paris" —and we left it at that.

The election was being conducted in a fair, serious way with people voting freely for their four different parties, and speeches from loud-speakers all about; and I lay in bed and read, and listened to the equally persistent cooing of the doves. It was pleasant to reach the open again after two days; to find old

Hasan with a horse, which he led on a halter through cornfields to the castle, or to the ancient Anemurium under the ruined fortifications of the cape. The cape itself drops sheer on its farther side, where the south pushes a breastwork of headlands, white and black, into the sea. In the lee of its eastern slope, the dead city is Roman and Byzantine, with no beauty left in theatre, odeon, or the place like a Piranesi print in whose shadowy arcades the goats are stabled on heaps of their own dung in the half-light. On the slope above are the dead steep streets of barrel-vaulted tombs, stuccoed and sometimes painted.

Another little river is here, carpeted with yellow and white water-flowers. It has wandered a hundred yards or so away from a deserted ancient bridge, lost in the corn. As we rode through these ripening harvests, Hasan with his hand caressed them, with a look of tenderness that made one feel the bond between the peasant and his earth; and the wind seemed to understand the long secret, and threw an equal light around us from the bending ridges, whether of the cornland or the sea.

On two other days we took a donkey up forest paths, to see ruins on the slopes of the Arymagdus valley—a naked western look-out fort called Bonjuluk, or the Bead, on the west slope, and a monastery or palace perhaps, called Yelbis Kalesi, above Daketüzü, on the east. It was unfortified, placed there perhaps for summer coolness. The windows of the upper storeys must have been arched and open, and the doorway not prepared for defence, nor was there anything strategic in its site, in spite of its fine view towards the north wind and the hills. As they told me that no Frank had been up there, I took its measurements very roughly, and from its tumble of fallen arches looked down the Sini valley, and up to the yayla, the summer camp of Daketüzü to which the villagers ride 'twelve hours with a donkey' when their harvests are gathered, and stay for the three summer months as they have probably done from the earliest times.

It was almost impossible to get a view of this building over-grown in its courts with old pines; but there was a pleasant feeling about it of living and leisure, above the threatened hurry and defence of the fortifiers on the plain. The winds were scented with resin and made a noise in the trees, and the shepherd girls and boys who haunt the ruins came about us, keeping their dogs in order and spinning their prickly wool. Women dress brightly in all this country, with the liveliest printed cottons that Europe can send them for open overskirts and trousers and quilted jackets, and they put on striped aprons and scarves of their own weaving round their waists. On their heads they wear a white cotton cloth with amulets or coins, and a high stuffing inside to make it tall: and when they go out they tuck it under their chins to make a wimple, and ride just as they did when the Crusaders saw them, with scarcely a change.

What I liked best in Anamur was the road from the river valley and bridge to the town, lined with harvests like the road of Shalott and with the same sort of traffic dotted along it, in little cavalcades of donkeys, or horses with foals, or people who looked like Canterbury pilgrims; or the bananas of Anamur (the only place in Turkey where they grow them) carried down on camels to the shore. The camels make a great ado with their forefeet, lifting them high as those of a stepping trotter and using all the muscles in an accomplished way, while the hind feet trail behind as best they can; and the boy with shaved head and rags tied together feels like a prince riding on his donkey at the head of a string of four of them, while his sister, with loose red boots and blue- and red-striped trousers and a skirt of flowered cotton, drags in the dust behind. Now and then, but rarely, a bus or lorry drives by, with its name— 'Flying Fortress' or 'Mashallah'—written upon it. The road dips through little corn-growing hills, and the embroidered saddle-bags show from far away. Calves and kids are scattered on green expanses, and camels that are not busy are browsing where the forests touch the ploughed lands of the plain.

I shall remember Anamur when many more comfortable places are forgotten: and its people too—Mustapha the driver, who walked with us up to Yelbis for fun and divided the egg I gave him with four shepherds (shaming me, who had eaten an entire one by myself). Or the old woman who came out from the cottage to offer a glass of water as she saw us passing in the hot hours of the day. Or the wedding near the lighthouse of Anemurium, wavering across country, with four bales and three chests on camels, and lamps and mirror and paper flowers, and the bride held on her horse by two male relatives, her head covered with a pink and silver cloth; and men in front and women behind on about thirty horses, with small drowsy children clasped on the saddle-bows, and a flute and drum.

I shall forget the hotel and its pains, and the crowd that gathered to watch my every mouthful at the door of the little restaurant, and shall remember the scent of orange blossom wafted from all the gardens through the city streets, and the unknown, sweet breezes from the fields and flowers. And the young school-teacher teaching himself English with a linguaphone. And the journalist who wanted an English wife.

A country looked at from the sea is like the sleeping Princess, the unknown. From the land it is no longer enchanted, but varied and human, a foundation for friendship and living. And perhaps it is a good way to come to know it when machinery breaks down and one is left marooned in a quiet place, one's own life suspended in a vacant interval that human variety can wander through at will.

4

CILICIAN DIGRESSION

Anamur to Antalya

Alexander now went towards Side, whose inhabitants are Cymaeans from Aeolian Cyme ... they forgot their native tongue and talked a foreign language straight away, and ... henceforward ... had been so many foreigners, contrary to the ways of their neighbours.

ARRIAN I, 26, 4.

AN EFFENDI AS FRESH AS WE WERE FRETTED KEPT US WAITING in Mustapha's jeep for three hours before we started. It was the Mustapha who had divided his egg with the shepherds, and he was an unassuming little man with a harmless look under a peaked cap worn as large as he could find. He stopped at a house in the outskirts of Anamur, where a wife more buxom and radiant than one would have expected brought out the last packages; and we were off—into country that returned to its loneliness as soon as we climbed out of the western edge of the Anamur plain. The cape, a squat rhinoceros bending its horn to sea, stood out behind us; and the road kept to the high houseless mountainsides. A little castle with arrow slits called, they said, Harakilise Arana, stood alone among pine-woods far below.

The mountains of Taurus run here level and unbroken, spouting springs and streams and falling steeply, and ancient names persisting show how little the land has changed; Mellesh is the Melissa of Strabo, and its few cottages and cascading slopes end in flat rocks in the water, where a little pier has been built for a local mine. Only pathways reach it. The next and other break is Charadrus, now Kaladeré, where a river flows between high pressing cliffs.

Even goats were rare on these high stretches: hoopoes in pairs and white-breasted wagtails had the landscape to themselves. The last trace of Anamur was a lime-kiln with blackened stones mounded on a small round tower, in which the village women fed a fire of thorns for five days and nights continuously. The men stood round piling it up, and it was shooting its flames into the sunlight. The next human meeting was a woman—blood streaming down her face—plodding like an animal, her baby on her back, and two men with a matter-of-fact air behind her. There had been a quarrel; the foreman of a group of road-menders a little farther on asked Mustapha to help, but he shrugged his shoulders: the eternal triangle was nothing to him in comparison to the jeep, which gave trouble. "It is the brake," he explained at the top of each narrow slope.

The engine got wet as we crossed the Kaladeré's flooded stream, and we let it drip while the policeman of the little village gave us tea. There are only two villages, one of sixty and one of eighty families, on either side of the river, with a ruined bridge at half an hour's walk up the valley, and a few tombs and a decayed *han* lost in the folds of the ground. Great cloud-ridden shoulders hemmed us in from north and east, the mount Andriclus of the ancients on the rocky shore called Platanistus, most of whose plane trees must have disappeared. Strabo mentions this place as a fortress and port, and it stretches into history in a small way before and after his time, being recorded by Hecataeus in the sixth century B.C.[1] and by the Crusaders in the twelfth A.D. They knew it as Calandro or Scalandro and mention it as the frontier between Armenians and Greeks in the journey of Philip Augustus, in 1191;[2] it was the country of Sir Adan, seneschal of the Armenians, whose lands lay between Seleuceia and Galonoros—the Crusaders' Candelore and modern Alanya.[3]

The tremendous landscape mounts again after Kaladeré, until it opens to steep but lower cultivated slopes, and looks on to a headland that opens as if the world ended, at the ruins of Antiocheia ad Cragum.

A Lusignan princess was brought here, carried off by a pirate from Cyprus where she and her children were bathing, and the Armenian king Leo freed and escorted her along the way we had travelled, to Amaury her husband who came for her across the sea. At that time when intermarryings were frequent, the Lusignans were half Armenian and their king, Peter I, in the 15th century, conquered Corycus and Antalya.[4] The traffic of the coast with Cyprus was important, and it was even closer in earlier ages. Antiocheia and Silifke, Arsinoe and Berenice, were the Hellenistic cities of the seaboard, built on easier ground to supersede the first Greek centres like Nagidus near Anamur, Celenderis or Holmi. Here Antiochus III sailed, before his fortune turned, first perhaps giving the name to Antiocheia and taking the other cities also one by one, till a Rhodian ultimatum reached him at Alanya and his troubles began. And, after he was defeated, the corn and gold of his tribute travelled, 'with more delays upon the journey than had been taken into account', from Syria to the Romans in Pamphylia by this road.[5]

Owing to the effendi, it was too late to walk to the promontory, and the very existence of its ruins was denied by a local shepherd till I climbed a little hillock and saw them where they were to be expected. This empty triumph was all I could hope for; the road turned inland and rain was threatening, and we now ran quickly through gentler country, by a stream parallel with the coast but separated by green hills. It led us to the Ghazi Pasha or Selinti river, that dries in summer, to a place where a double ford divides it and leads to Ghazi Pasha along an easy road. Cases of bananas from tidy plantations were stacked here, waiting for lorries; and even at Kaladeré, which lorries do not reach, there is now a plantation. The fruit is taken off in motor-boats and sent to Istanbul from Antalya, and there is no intermediate landing-place, either at Cragus or Selinti.

Parvisque Syedris,
Quo portu, mittitque rates recipitque Selinus.[6]

Those days are over, and Ghazi Pasha was in that state of squalor between civilizations which may come upon us all at any moment. There was nowhere in particular to sleep. Mustapha considered the hotel to be below even the standard of Anamur, and a young man who cooked our meal, and was the postmaster's wife's nephew, took me to a little house filled with women—sisters, grandmothers, aunts, wife, mother-in-law and nieces, who gave me a quilt and mattress with great kindness, and left me to rest in their parlour.

I have come to know such rooms well, for they all resemble each other in their combination of embroidery and bareness, lace curtains and fancy pelmets, hard benches with bolsters worked in cross-stitch by girls before they marry, cushions like bullets, niches for Qurans or school-books, and *kilims* on the floor. The Quran was in its niche in a white crocheted case, and a Hollywood star above it, because of the nearness of the two cinemas of Alanya. But the life itself takes a good many years of a new road before it changes, and the latest cement-built shops are cubes in a row with doors at the back to their store-rooms in the Greco-Roman pattern; and the kindness in the household, the serving of guests as if it were a part of religion (which it is), and the mobile quality of the furniture with absence of cupboards or bedsteads, or even tables in any quantity, so that any number can be accommodated anywhere—all this still belongs to a deeply-rooted world.

As we sat in the evening, with shoes off in the way of the east, and the postmaster and his nephew comfortably relaxed in their own harim, I noticed how much the Turk suffers from the fact that a traveller nearly always sees him in public trying to do the women's work. The things that make life gay when women see to them are attended to 'by the hands of strangers', while wives sit dumb, with an unbecoming loose coat and a kerchief over the head, trying not to be noticed. This is custom, and has nothing to do with the religion of Islam. In a mixed Muslim place, like Iskenderun, the Arab elegance is visible at once even in the poor Alaouites from across the border; the femininity of the Levant is kept indoors there, but only to be more fit for pleasure; its clothes and easy contours are made to go to bed with, and the women, when this age is over, think no longer of their appearance and do not, in fact, try to please in any other way. But while their tide is with them, the young women's veiling is royal; protected like idols, they breathe security and move with enviable safety in a walled world, with anything but submission in their seclusion. They are set apart, yet they remain individual and are not destroyed. But the Turks have a middle-class Victorian attitude to their harim and expect it to be there to serve them, with a constant feeling that women are not complete entities in themselves. The peasants make them work more heavily than they do in Arabia, and civilization, which requires feminine time and attention, seems to suffer and decline where women work very hard. Yet even here the home feeling is pleasant after the dingy world of men. And especially so since the Turk—in spite of his strength and self-reliance—is dull. He is as different from the Arab as anyone can be, even physically, with his good head, neither long nor broad but sanely balanced, and capable safe hands and general regularity of feature, compared to the long Beduin hands and swinging movements and faces furrowed with emotions that belong to the nomad lands, at any rate, of Arabia.

Unlike the Arab, who cares for nothing else, the Turk is not interested in the abstract. The abstract, that interprets the world and makes it no longer impenetrable and impervious, and is reached by curiosity one step beyond our borders, means nothing to him. The Arab, with his tiresomeness, is an artist. To him the unknown world *is real*.

And women and artists, wherever they may be, are always pushed a little way over that abstract edge, since the two ends of life—the greatest and the smallest—are in their hands. The unknown exists for them: and, for this reason, the woman's side of the house was always an indescribable improvement on the dreariness of the man-made hotel.

Selinti was called Trajanopolis when Trajan died there, and its ruins are near the mouth of the Inje-kara, the Ghazi Pasha river, a short way by jeep and another half-hour's walk over flat arable land from the village. Mustapha had to carry me across the stream, which ran here divided in three full but shallow courses. A long aqueduct reached it with denuded arches, and the ruins leaned against a cliff nearly five hundred feet high. A path led to a fortress at the top, and some ancient stonework showed; but it looked poor, and my time was short, and the summits of Taurus threatening; and already a water-spout, a vertical white fountain out at sea, was moving towards us. The lower ruins, Roman and late, were grouped round the square space of Trajan's memorial, of which the bases only of one hundred and ten columns are left; and in the necropolis was the endless sameness of tombs—those small, self-satisfied congregations going back so unchanged and so far. "Jerusalem is a gossipy place," said the wife of a bishop when her daughter was going out there without gloves; and conformity, bridging the ages in its threadbare way, seems worse among the dead.

History had come and gone, but what history, I thought, could stand up to such a stream of mediocrity and oblivion, such depths upon depths of silence so feebly interrupted? Through centuries the young, at all events, must have longed for variety, even for thunderbolts and pirates. In such negative surroundings even war, even the sack of cities will be faced.

Ghazi Pasha

Good administration is not enough, if boredom, like the Red
Queen's biscuit, makes the thirsty stretches, the slow repetitions,
the lifelong span of Eastern space and time, seem even more
monotonous than they are. In Asia, or anywhere else for
that matter, a spice of drama should always be added, if we do
not wish to see people insert it independently into the sameness
of their lives at our expense.

At the postmaster's house the girls and children came out of
school, and kissed their mother's hand, and raised it to their
forehead. Their tradition is pleasant on its road to the final
monotony, and they treat old age as agreeably as they can.
"You are old; we are young," Mustapha and his friends had
been repeating, like a chorus, when we scrambled over ruins;
and in the house, the whole chain of human relationships was
complete. The grandmother had never left Ghazi Pasha, and
could not read; the mother, with a beautiful Rembrandt face,
told how they had worked at the new Latin letters and "studied
for a week to write Ada, Adam". She had borne ten children
and eight had died; there was neither road nor doctor at that
time, and it took three days to reach Alanya. Now there is a
school with three girl-teachers, who find their own lodgings
and live on 150 Turkish lira monthly for their first two years.
They were dressed with such bits of modern fashion as Ghazi
Pasha encouraged; and the old world and the new were on
friendly terms. It was a tolerant place, and regretted the
Greeks who had lived here (as all along this coast) before the
1922 disasters. There had been friends among them, they told
me; and I came away feeling that not Pandora, but some
Ideology probably first opened the box of troubles; and that
Ghazi Pasha and the little places like it are doing their best in a
blind way to heal the wound.

The rain poured down next day. Mustapha closed the jeep
as well as he could, and I had no heart to photograph a practic-
ally invisible landscape, or to hunt for Laertes where the

biographer came from, or for Syedra, where Pompey paused in his flight. The Taurus, that rises here to over five thousand feet, was still hidden; the road, no longer steep over headlands, was dull; and it took us two and a half instead of one and a half hours to reach Alanya because the jeep's whole footboard, with its brake, jerked up at intervals towards the driver. Mustapha finally took a screw from somewhere else and screwed it down, with unimpaired good temper; in spite of all the things that happen to their cars I have never heard a driver in Asia use an impatient word to a machine. Watching while the rain splashed him with a halo, I wondered, for the thousandth time, whether it is better to be resourceful, or to do away with the necessity for resource and replace a screw in time. This great question may involve the future of our species; but luckily I need not decide it, and darkness and our arrival in Alanya put an end to meditation in a clean, tidy and newly-built hotel.

The adventurous part of this trip was over, since Alanya is within the present tourist orbit of Turkey, and visited by most travellers who reach the south. A good road runs to it, almost level from the smooth Pamphylian bay. It was sometimes held to be the boundary between Pamphylia and Cilicia, and in its time, even more than Seleuceia, it was a centre for pirates, the last to defy Pompey. At a later date Diodatus Tryphon held out here against Antiochus VII, the Seleucid king. But the great period of Alanya was that of the Karamanlis, when ten Turcoman Emirs divided the Seljuk lands. It was then, in A.D. 1333, that Ibn Batuta landed, and found that Candelore, as it was called, was the chief port of the coast together with Antalya and Lajazzo, Ayas, busy with the export of timber to Egypt. It was from Candelore and from Antalya that Syrian and Egyptian merchants would cross Asia Minor by the inland ways from which Christians were excluded, and even in 1403, when the decline was beginning, Marshal Boucicaut saw the place filled with goods and trading with Cyprus, which helped it against the Ottomans till the final defeat in 1471. Under the new dynasty, Candelore and Satalia (Antalya) became the main ports for the slave trade. Hundreds were packed in Greek ships from Gallipoli or Adrianople, or were carried by the Italians from the Black Sea direct. About two thousand were sent to Cairo in the year, taxed in transit by the Genoese at Haifa, who sometimes exempted Christian slaves.[7]

This is the sad facet of history: but the happy side of Alanya belongs to the beauty of Alaeddin's city, which gives it its stamp and outlives all the other ages—ancient, Ottoman, or Crusading—that encrust the fortified pyramid on its hill. Beyond all military architectures, the early Greek and the Seljuk seem to me to express the delight of their building. Functional as they are—for they allow no unessential to mislead them—they refuse to be limited to economic terms: they reach their perfection regardless of expense or effort, and a sort of radiance inevitably follows, as if the axle of immortality ran through them. An absence of triviality, a depth and fearlessness triumphant over fashion is reached by all such works—the Greek wall, the Seljuk tower, the wing of the jet fighter, and all the inventions that grasp life so neatly and joyfully that death ceases to matter in the count.

This is excellence for its own sake, which our economic states degrade in favour of minor equalities. Surrounded by second-rate comforts, we watch our art and words, our loves themselves—deteriorate and our joy depart. But in all paths that seem permanent, we find this delight as a signpost, and what pain goes with it is accepted. 'For thus my goddess Mother telleth me, Thetis the silver-footed, that twain fates are bearing me to the issue of death.'[8] In spite of all, the echo never dies, and even its eccentric expressions are engaging. Young good-looking Mr. Cockerell, who had been staying with Canning at the Embassy in Pera, got off his ship at Troy to run naked three times round the tumulus of Achilles, remembering Alexander, and proving that the main thoroughfare persists.

The arsenal that houses Alaeddin's galleys, and the walls that embrace Alanya with battlements and gates, all possess this quality of the Seljuks, whose enjoyment happened to be centred on the art of war.

The tower built by an Arab of Aleppo in A.D. 1265 has been repaired and this makes it look slightly like a gasometer at present, but will be helpful for future generations; and nothing can take away the geometric ingenuity of its pattern, different on every one of its five storeys, with windows narrowed towards the outside for the safety of the bowmen, and arches that break from the central pillar like leaves from a stalk. The harbour below is quiet; the fishermen's nets hang on the quay, and eaves and overhanging windows of old houses surround them; and one weekly steamer needles in and out along the southern capes.

It is quiet enough while the modern streets are approaching and 'next year' I was told, 'all the markets will be new'. I had the usual difficulty in photographing the shop where everything hangs on nails along the doorposts, while Ghalib Bey, who directs the touristry of Alanya, tried to stop me with promises of cement next year. Every Turk, he kept on saying, loves strangers and is brave. True as I have found this, it gave me a feeling of unreality to hear it so often repeated; and it must, I felt, be bad for people to think virtue so geographical; but it was no use explaining. I deflected Ghalib to the five-hundred-feet climb of the ramparts, about which a middle-aged guide anywhere else would have made a fuss. But Ghalib has kept his reserves of toughness, and with a plump friend, a merchant of oranges from Istanbul, who joined our party, we turned under a pointed gateway to the old-fashioned part of the town.

The galley slips that Alaeddin built to carry on the pirate

tradition are on the beach here, still seen in use by Colonel Leake in 1800 when 'vessels they call girlangich (or swallow), with three masts and a bowsprit and triangular sails', were being built. Nothing is left now except a few fishing-boats with nets and gourds in five long spaces, under vaulted arches that end with a moulding on the naked walls. The sea laps their twilight, and they keep their fine and gallant air. We climbed from them by a wall overrun with gardens, through the steep half-desolate houses of the town which the Greeks in 1922 abandoned, to the eastern rampart that zigzags on the lip of a precipice and falls out of sight into the sea. As we toiled up the steps in a narrow sort of safety, Ghalib continued to paint the future of Alanya, tinted by Monte Carlo and Miami, places to which he is sent to see how things are done. He brings back ideas of hotels and promenades to replace the houses by the harbour: small hotels, I begged, and trained young men to run them, not one giant *Palas* with six amateurs lounging at the bottom of the stairs. Ghalib scarcely heard, but turned with his saga to the orange-merchant, who was glad of any excuse to sit on a stone and perspire; till Ghalib spurred him for another hundred steps or so by saying that "all the tourists come this way".

The cross-wall of the citadel almost immediately contradicted him, intersecting us without any sign of steps or ladder to get down by, and we looked with anxiety at the slightly but not sufficiently uneven meeting of the Seljuk walls. If at all possible, and however difficult, I meant to climb them; and, again to my surprise, the Istanbul merchant showed no reluctance: we slid, and soon found a hole by which to enter the compound of the citadel itself.

In this inner space were houses in gardens, a poor, pleasant suburb round a small Seljuk mosque; and beyond, through more walls, the fortress enclosure, with fallen vaults of store-rooms, a brick-cistern into which the few women about here still dip their buckets, and a charming Byzantine chapel with faded external niches round the drum.

Here too beyond the walls on the sea-cliff is the lighthouse, whitewashed and very clean; and, six hundred feet or so straight down, a medieval chapel on a thin ridge near the water's edge. Across the bay, Feis Dagh is ridged against the eastern Taurus; in the west the coast flattens to the far Chelidonian headlands; and close below, the little harbour with a new-built pier is neat as a toy. We walked down in the evening light and I felt that months, or even a year, might easily pass in Alanya. On either side of the promontory are long and sandy beaches; there are comfortable houses full of odd gable windows deep in the orange-scented gardens of the plain. The new town with white houses flattens out into suburbs under a fine grey pencil minaret, newly built; and the old city itself, half-empty, too steep for traffic, with cobbled streets that dive beneath the houses, is quieter than country, as if turned back in memory to all the footsteps whose echoes have died away. The promontory's shadow lay across the sea, and we walked down by the Osmanli mosque which two men were repairing; by the *turbe* or tomb of Sultan Bey, whose hospital is there too, built eighty years or so after the Seljuks and shape-lessly ruined; through the city gate of the more ancient Cora-cesium with its straight classic lintel; and the lower, beautiful carved Gothic of the Seljuk, where the defences were most accessible and strong.

When I made my way for supper the *lokanta* was already crowded and, having looked vainly for an empty table, I sat down beside a young engineer from Istanbul. I had not yet seen a woman sitting in public since I left Mersin, and finally asked him, in the course of conversation, how Turkish ladies eat when they travel. "A married woman does not travel," he said, in some surprise.

This, I since discovered, is old-fashioned; but the women in these remoter districts do usually have their meals brought up to them, cold but in comfort, to their rooms.

Next morning, the jeep promised for Antalya had left to work in the forest, but the Forestry Department produced a kind assistant director, who was going my way. The day was cloudy and dark, the road's mountain beauty hidden, and there was no very obvious interest along the level coast except for a Seljuk tithe-barn or store-house, alone at Sharapsa in a field. A severe undivided rectangle, battlemented, with eleven buttresses each side and arrow-slits between them, and one fine door, it was as military in its way as the arsenal of Alanya. It is now a stable, its long barrel-vaulted interior divided by arches that do not reach the ground, and it is on the north of the road, in sight, near the ancient Ptolomeis.

Small cities were strung out on this coast, and their ruins are among the scrub, with the stucco washed away that made them pleasant, and little left but a rubble of decay. Like a constant series of unnecessary remarks, they spoil the landscape, and I felt that in any case the Forestry director might not wish to stop too often on his way. But when we reached Manavgat, and paused for a glass of tea under the plane trees by the river, I persuaded him to take me to Side, which is only five miles off the road. There we found the Grecian world again—a land spread gently. From the portals of Taurus, the rich smooth streams came pouring; and aqueducts arched across miles of tillage, and some forgotten column might be found there, lying anywhere at random in the corn.

The arcades of the theatre rose from their solitude of thorns and brambles; the lost columned streets and houses, the fountain wall that spouted through three openings under marble garlands, the trophies, pediments, and walls, the court already, in the 3rd or 4th century A.D.,[9] encircled with domes like a mosque, the Byzantine doors and cloisters whose statues have fallen from their niches, the bases of marble temples that stood against the sea: all is there in fragments, but easy, under the superficial ground or in the familiar air. White foam breaks on the mole that in dark and broken fragments holds the city harbour, a silted shoal; and on the small museum terrace the statues, all in pieces, look out over winglike empty curves of sand.

The middle age is forgotten—the Crusaders crossing the mountains 'like quadrupeds with hands and feet',[10] carried sick in litters or on the shields of their squires over the precipices of Calycadnus; the Seljuks who slipped their thin boats like hunting panthers from the fine walls of Alanya and flew their flags at Anamur. But Side, whose language was so mixed that no one understood it, who became notorious for her dealings with pirates and sold their prisoners for them by public crying in her streets—she in her time acquired the Greek secret, and even her ruins are alive. Mehmet Bey, the assistant director, felt it as I did, and walked about overwhelmed and ecstatic, unable to put his feeling into words. We forgot that he was Turkish and I English; that we could neither of us express any of the things we really felt in each other's language; we were held by what in its day had held the known world before us from Scotland to India and the people of Side themselves, whatever their alien sources—a civilization which in spite of cruelties and errors can never be superseded, since even the merest trifles it has left us, the siting of its buildings, the stray stones of its walls, the fragments of its marbles, hold that strong thread of immortality we are in danger of forgetting, our only home and native country in this world.

Part II

PAMPHYLIA

Leaving Phaselis, Alexander sent part of his force through the mountain passes towards Perge.

ARRIAN I, 26, 1.

In a land most rich, under a sky most kindly, among natives mild in disposition, all that fierceness with which they came has grown gentle.

LIVY XXXVIII, 17, 17.

5

THE PAMPHYLIAN PLAIN

Alexander left a guard at Side and went on to Syllium, a fortified place with a garrison of mercenaries and also of the natives of those parts. But he could not take it in his stride, and, besides . . . the Aspendians . . . had shut their gates upon his envoys, and were repairing weak places in their walls. Learning this, Alexander marched towards Aspendus.

ARRIAN I, 26, 5.

THE LATEST OF THE PAMPHYLIAN CITIES WAS FIRST CALLED Attaleia from Attalus of Pergamum its founder, and then Satalya in the Middle Ages; and it seems not to have existed in the days of Alexander, though it became the chief port of the country very quickly and eventually took over the Aspendus trade in salt, oil, wool and corn. All through the Middle Ages, till the end of the Crusades, it was famous for its harbour, described by Ibn Batuta and Yakut before him, who calls it the chief port of Rum, where the Crusaders embarked for Palestine. When Ibn Batuta landed in the 14th century, the Seljuk Kilij Arslan had built a palace on the cliffs, and every trade had its own street and market; and the Christian quarter climbed steeply round the port, shut in by a wall whose gates were closed at night and during Friday prayers. The Turcoman princes, pressed by the Osmanlis, needed Egyptian support as they did at Alanya, and they loaded their ships for Cairo with slaves, Turkish and Christian, and timber and pitch, until Peter I of Cyprus held Antalya for twelve years from A.D. 1361, and the inland trade stopped for a time. Tamerlane captured it for twenty-five years, and in the 15th century Adalia, or Satalya, lost its western commerce, though wax, honey and saffron, gum tragacanth for which Pisidia was famous, sesame, Vallonia acorns, silk, fine wool, red leather, carpets and slaves continued to be sent to Muslim ports like Alexandria and Damietta. The Christians worked in the city's shipyards, building large galleys or slimmer craft for the pirates, while from Cairo broadcloths were imported from the west. Even in 1800, Antalya was considered one of the best governments in Anatolia; Beaufort saw it with ditch, double wall and square towers; with Hadrian's splendid gate, that still exists, walled up with fourteen columns; and the port enclosed by piers whose towers have gone. A third of its eight thousand inhabitants were Greeks who spoke only Turkish, and its prosperity at this time was due to the demand of the British Levantine garrisons for wheat during the Napoleonic wars.[1]

But when Alexander descended from Lycia and broke into the Pamphylian plain, the only community established on this shore was that of Olbia, in the western corner. His army crossed the mountain while he, with a small company, followed the edge of the sea; and both must have met and rested for a night at least in the territory of this priest-state, of which nothing is left, unless possibly a few holes in a low rock-face may mark it, where the Arabis Su trickles unobtrusively to sea. The lonely coast is haunted with lost names west of Antalya: Thebe and Lyrnessos are there—the tribes of Briseis and of Andromache far from her Mysian home, whose father was 'King of the men of Kilikia'. Perhaps they rebuilt their cities after vague wandering to the south. Homeric echoes remained, and the Arcadian Greek was spoken; and Atreus–Atarissyas was recorded, and Phaselis, which gave its name to the little boat ennobled by Catullus, treasured Achilles' spear.[2]

All this is now an almost uninhabited mountain corner, frowned on by the ridges of Termessus and crossed by its torrents. The Macedonians marched along it, by the lowest of the limestone shelves that gently terrace Pamphylia towards the hills, where old presses for oil lie about in numbers of places now uncultivated and idle. Here and there across the stony levels, at the back of La'ara for instance, one may find channels cut in rock five or six metres deep and five or six feet broad, bridged by roughly-shaped boulders, where the laborious water runs tunnelled for many miles.

The rivers that provide these waters are mostly wasted, for they cut too deep for irrigation and only the goats climb down by zigzag millennial stone-cut crannies, and drink where the shadows wreathe themselves in with the stream. Useful or no, every water of Pamphylia is beautiful, whether it be the Termessus torrent that dries round its islands in summer; or Kirk-göz at the foot of the passes, spilling lakes among water-lilies for coot and heron; or Düden, the ancient Catarrhactes, that spouts out of two holes in the floor of the plain, and widens under its long crooked bridge in marshy mirrors, and throws itself east of Antalya over honeycomb cliffs into the sea. There is Cestrus, the White River of Perge; and Eurymedon under the acropolis of Aspendus, that carried fleets and battles and reflects bridges built by Seljuk, Byzantine and Roman, broken or entire, and carries timber from forests of the ridges of Selge; and Melas, the modern Manavgat, the most majestic of all, that from its scarcely travelled gorges pours a smooth green flood into the sun.

These all flow parallel; and the ancient cities drew them off and banked their waters between stone or marble parapets, at any rate in later days. One can see their work in Perge and in Lagon, an obscure small place on the way to Termessus, where water-courses built up to run along the tops of walls are being cleared, rather destructively, by the peasants, and the old canal decorated with altars runs straight through a ploughed field.

Lower down on the same line is a Roman bridge humped over a canal. But mostly, as the ancient world lost itself in the Arab wars, the water-channels dwindled, and cultivation died, and smaller reservoirs were built for local use—the domed buildings so common in Caria, or walled-in underground steps that lead to a spring. The water pattern shrank into dots instead of lines; and so did the life of the countryside, with hamlets disappearing, until the Seljuk victory of Manzikert brought the nomads—the chief and only real change in the life of Anatolia.[3] They roamed over what had been fields, and the olive went wild and the pine took hold of the stony terraces, where one stumbles on the walls and tombs of places unrecorded, uninhabited and forgotten. Their markets make useful patches, big enough for the shrunken harvests of today.

One such is reached through gate-posts hewn in the natural rock-wall, above Örenköy and the ridge where the Düden river springs out of the ground. Pisidian probably, then Roman-Greek with a square tower and later tombs, then declining with untidy building, it looks over the plain and its cities—Antalya, Perge, Aspendus, Sillyon and Side—and north to wooded landscapes open and to all appearances empty, where—a villager told me—"ruined places are thick under the trees". The stony track was a market road, or 'pazarlik' in the time of his father's father; and the water came in conduits from the pass.

A good road now reaches Antalya, and lorries bring prosperity and cultivation, with a trade in early vegetables for Ankara. The countryside has probably returned more or less to what it was in the matter of tillage, for at no time can cultivation have covered the rocky soil of the plain entirely.

Aspendus was known for the breeding of horses, and Alexander requisitioned the stock held there for the Persian king; and this alone shows that wild patches for grazing existed, even when the olive groves were at their richest in the land.

There is no notice of little harbours like La'ara, whose mole and Roman ruins stand at the cliffs' end where the smooth shore begins that runs to the Cilician border.

Alexander did not go so far, but made for Perge, which was friendly. Having negotiated a tribute with Aspendus, and having occupied the important harbour of Side with a garrison which remained there, he turned from the rough Cilicia and marched north-west under the walls of Sillyon.

These Pamphylian citadels are all in sight of one another on separate and isolated hills.

Near the present Murtana, the Alexandrian Perge has been destroyed on its flat acropolis. The temple of Artemis—a dark pillared church in the late Middle Ages—is used as a stable today. It was already desecrated when Cicero described Diana 'stripped and plundered' by Verres, and the gold from the statue itself 'pulled off and taken'.[4] Like many of the coastal places, Perge descended when the seas grew safe under Rome, and built its walls and towers in the plain; a circular gate with marble seats and statues, a water-channel ridged to make the curving waves shine, a theatre, a stadium sloping on vaulted apses—they remain among suburbs lost in crops.

This was the metropolis of Pamphylia in which St. Paul preached on his way to Antalya:[5] but it has nothing to do with Alexander. Even the river, once navigable under the acropolis seven miles from the sea, has shifted to the east, and left a dry and shallow western valley. Nothing but a few scraps of wall and many stone sarcophagi crowded shoulder to shoulder below the slope remind one of the pilgrims' way to our Lady of Perge, and its yearly festival and widespread worship.

Aspendus (Balkiz) is also out of the way of pirates some

seven miles up the once navigable Eurymedon; not that this kept it safe, for Cimon won his naval battle beneath its walls in 467 B.C., and Thrasybulus was killed and his ships and unruly soldiers chased away in 390. Tissaphernes in 411 B.C. stationed his fleet here, and the Rhodians two-and-a-quarter centuries later, when they defeated Hannibal, put into the river with thirty-two quadriremes and four triremes.[6] Here too, as in Perge, the long-collected riches were looted by the Romans. 'You are aware, gentlemen,' said Cicero, in his exposure of the miseries of Asia, 'that Aspendus is an old and famous town in Pamphylia, full of fine statuary. I shall not allege that from this town this or that particular statue was removed. My charge is that Verres did not leave one single statue behind; that from temples and public places alike, with the whole of Aspendus looking on, they were all openly loaded on wagons and carted away. Yes, even the famous Harpist of Aspendus, about whom you have often heard the saying that is proverbial among the Greeks . . . that "he made his music inside"—him too he carried off.'[7]

The Empire made up for these outrages with a long era of peace, and the theatre of Aspendus was dedicated to Marcus Aurelius and Verus. It is the most perfect of its age that remains, and stands with scarcely anything structural missing, built for seven thousand five hundred spectators, with the latest devices of its age still there, such as a racked sounding-board to improve the acoustics. The looted statues of the town were replaced by many new ones, in tiers of niches on the stage, and the barbarous Roman shows came to be shown here, as well as traditional plays. Traces of its use have now been found in Seljuk days.

Behind it the acropolis is a flat-topped oval like all these hills—outposts, in the plain, of the main body of Taurus, whose summits above their shadows, are endlessly restless, like a line of pikes and scimitars on the northern horizon. An aque-

duct comes down to the plain from that sharp-pointed Renais-
sance background, reaches the maximum height of its stone-
cut channel on two rows of arches one above the other, and
curves towards the acropolis in vast and ruined piers. On
the height itself, the nymphaeum, basilica, and markets show
the structure of Imperial Rome. Aspendus, the oldest of the
inland cities with a name on its coins, was barbarian in the 5th
century B.C. though it claimed descent from Argos; but there
is nothing left in sight now to remind one of things earlier
than the Caesars.

Between the town and the river, where Alexander camped
within the outer wall among the little houses, the theatre stands
on flat ground, like a box from which the lid has been lifted.
Proud, limited, and magnificent, there is a prison air about it—
a difference as of death and life that one feels between the
Roman and the Greek. No landscape stretches here beyond
a low and unobtrusive stage, for the easy coming and going of
the gods. Human experience, that moved with freedom and
mystery, is here walled-in with balconies and columns; its
pure transparency, the far horizon window, is lost.

In the Greek theatre, with its simple three-doored stage
and chorus undertone of sorrow, the drama of life could
penetrate, without any barrier between them, the surrounding
vastness of the dark. I have listened to the Hippolytus of
Euripides in Epidaurus where the words of Artemis and
Aphrodite with the mountain pines and the sunset behind them,
become a limpid fear—a play no longer, but nature and all
that ever has been, anguish and waste of days, speaking to men.

This fluid universe stepped out of the world of Homer, and
enabled him to use the word *sacred* easily and rightly, for the
usual task of the sentinel or the common revolution of the day.
There is no difference, no closing away from nature, when
Hector's face appears 'like sudden night', or Agamemnon
groans from the deep of his heart like 'the maker of rain, or

hail, or snow sprinkled on the ploughed lands, or the fashioning of the wide mouth of bitter war'. That magnamimous use of the simile is no mere literary device, but an awareness of underlying harmony, a disregard of unreal essentially unexisting barriers between one thing and another, a freedom of movement between nature and man.

The echo of it was strong in Alexander, who kept his Iliad in the jewelled casket of Darius and thought of Achilles as himself. A great part of his disregard of death must have been cherished by the reading of Homer. 'It is a lovely thing to live with courage, and to die, leaving behind an everlasting renown' ... 'for if I abide here and besiege the Trojans' city, my returning home is taken from me, but my fame shall be imperishable; but if I go home to my dear native land, my life shall endure ...' It is the same voice separated merely by time and person, nor is it ever said that Alexander, even in his last illness, met death with reluctance: his choice, like that of Achilles, was made, and Hephaestion, his Patroclus, was dead. Many other things one can trace in part to Homer—as the feeling for the nobility of kingship: 'seeing that no common honour pertaineth to a sceptred king to whom Zeus apportioneth glory,' 'for proud is the soul of heaven-fostered kings, because their honour is of Zeus.' And it does not seem impossible, when Alexander leaped over the wall of Mallus alone among his enemies, that the thought came into his mind of Sarpendon of Lycia, dragging away the battlement of the Achaians and calling, where he stood alone on the wall, to his men to follow.[8]

Leaving the theatre of Aspendus and the Roman age to all its implications, we can imagine the flat land by the river filled, when Alexander came there, with gardens and small houses surrounded by a feeble wall; and the acropolis appearing—from Arrian's description—higher and fiercer than it is, because of the grandeur, perhaps, of the hills behind it—for it is certainly not very tall now and scarcely overlooks the theatre's height.

Alexander had no taste for useless sieges. He had taken over the Persian naval power down the coast, and his business there was ended: his next necessity was to open up a way to his base in Phrygia. The Aspendians, therefore, were able to get terms not very much harder than before, though—chiefly interested in their feuds with Perge, and reasonably free under Persia—they had already closed their gates and gathered their stuff from the fields when Alexander and his army appeared. What they can have found left out at the end of winter I cannot imagine. The Macedonians then returned to Perge, and left Sillyon which they had passed on their march to Aspendus, alone of the Pamphylian cities free and untouched on its hill. To visit it, a turn-off leads from the coast road, by the village of Abdurrahmanlar about twenty kilometres east of Antalya.

I drove there when the flocks were out and the asphodel in flower, and the Abdurrahmanlar elders gave me as a guide a young man who happened to be in charge of the D.D.T.-ing of five neighbouring parishes against malaria. We drove as far as we could, and then walked for half an hour and, passing through a later and lower city, climbed by a buttressed slanting track under a tower, through the place of a vanished gateway, to the flat acropolis.

The later inhabitants intersected it with a wall, and lived as well as they could in the southern portion, cluttering up their ancient monuments and lovely doorways in a rubble of small Byzantine stones; and the northern city now lay as if drowned in bushes, with column and arch, patterns of streets and stone-cut runnels of water scarcely visible under the criss-cross shadows of twigs the goats were nibbling, their delicate round muzzles fastidiously inserted among the thorns.

A goatherd in a black woollen cap, with moccasins cross-gartered like Malvolio, sat spinning in the sun. The village men all do this, and walk about with hanks of black or white wool wound on the left forearm, which they pull at and twist while they talk, and spin enough thread, the goatherd said (but I did not believe him) to make a tent in a fortnight. Sometimes they knit, with a hook at the end of one of their four needles, and turn out the white patterned stockings that look so well. Down below, in the Roman city, the goatherd's wife was visible, in front of a thatched hut patched with petrol tins, with four children about her; she too was outside in the spring sunshine, cleaning tinned yaourt pails that shone like silver from far away. The goatherd looked at us in a friendly manner with his green eyes, left his fifty goats browsing, and led us to the torso of a Roman soldier carved in marble, and over the city, which was his since no other human being was left to share it.

Palaces, and a public building with arched Byzantine windows still stand in the southern town and remind one that Sillyon was a bishopric when Perge and Aspendus had long been deserted. Its steep defensible sides no doubt made it the metropolis of Pamphylia. The fine early stone and straight lintels patterned with spirals are let in among rough medieval walls, and an early façade with six straight doors is on the south-west side, with an underground store-house, not far below, where the goatherd and his friends had found some blackened seeds of corn. To the south, a theatre is dug in above the precipice. Earthquakes have split it, but the rows of its seats are in order, and overlook cornfields between ridges of asphodel and grassland, and the Roman town, and the sea five miles away.

From these places the Greek mercenaries and native soldiers and the people whose language was still barbarian for all the city's Hellenizing ways, watched the Macedonian army as it marched between them and the sea and disappeared in the direction of Side, and as it returned under their high walls and

stored harvests, and marched away again towards Aspendus
and the west—fifteen thousand men or so, enough to raise a
dust among the olives and the stubble. Little else is known
of the city, except this glance of Alexander's as he passes. The

streets and palaces and houses of all its different ages lie voiceless
and contented in the sun.

When we reached my taxi, we sat on the grass among
asphodel stalks taller than ourselves, and lunched in a cool
breeze that blows in the afternoon in summer. Mindful of the

egg, at Anamur, that had to be divided among five, I now brought better provisions for stray encounters, and the guide and goatherd shared the meal, which was all the return I could offer for their kindness. Even so, they began to eat only when they felt sure I had finished, though I was able to press sweets for the children into the goatherd's hand. When we returned there, the village of Abdurrahmanlar gave coffee, and showed a coin of the helmeted Athena which it would not part with; and I drove back to Antalya in the evening to my home in the Jumhuriyet Hotel.

I came to know the town well as the weeks passed. Fairly early in the morning, for the spring was already warm here in the south, I would wander through the half-deserted streets of the old Christian quarter, superseded now by Muslim building. It also is decaying, but there are still houses under brown roofs pleasantly tucked away behind high walls in gardens, or opening on to narrow cobbled neglected streets with bay windows overhanging, where the name of Allah or some Turkish arabesque is painted on the peeling stucco, and wooden lattices, leaning out in a pear-shaped curve, let the women look up and down their street at ease.

There is a tarmac road to the harbour, over which an irrepressible Antalya waterfall gushes and splashes, making it almost impossible for horses; but it is pleasanter, if walking, to take the steep way in the shade, under the arch of one of the gates that used to be closed at nightfall, to the quays whose tranquillity is scarcely rippled by the American Navy or the weekly steamer.

Or one can find, down many steps, the beach where a lighter or two is building, among pots full of glue and smells of tar and drying nets hung like the sails round the huts and bleached ships at Troy. This place is shaded by tall plane trees and high medieval walls with ancient foundations, which one meets here and there all over the town in unexpected corners,

with a bath or tomb built into them, or merely supporting sheds and gardens, in streets so quiet that the people who live there can bring their chairs in summer and sit out undisturbed. Near the eastern end of this quarter is the cathedral — a five-aisled basilica of the 6th or 7th century adapted from earlier work and touched up again in the 12th century with paint and stucco. Neglected now and forlorn, it still wears, like the real lace of a decayed gentlewoman, some piece of fine carved marble here and there. Mr. Daniell, who climbed up into the mountains and discovered Selge and died of malaria, was buried here by the two young naval officers, his companions, a hundred years ago; but I was unable to discover his tomb.

The east of the town, beyond a round Venetian tower, ends in municipal gardens full of flowers, which the Turks love. They grow them along the water that runs in a channel in the pleasant forgotten fashion of Perge, down the middle of the street; and round the post office, and in fact wherever they can. These things are all on the cliff-top, where the old city also extended, for the triple gate of Hadrian is there among the spidery, dusty cabs or *droskys*, whose horses' heads droop into their nosebags through the day. The taxis have another more central station, and behave like all taxis anywhere, except at funerals, when they press on their klaxons and move slowly, with an unbroken noise, right through the town. But the *droskys* wake up towards sunset, and move to and fro at an ambling pace for the people of Antalya who like to drive from one end of the town to the other. I shall never hear the clip-clop of hooves with that leisurely rhythm, without seeing the broad empty esplanade below my terrace window and the carriages and horses beribboned for Bairam driving one behind the other, their owners gazing into space with the same far-away expression with or without a fare. To get in, one had to pull them out of their day-dream by almost committing suicide under their wheels.

The most alluring of the Antalya conveyances were the buses, which also trotted to and fro along this thoroughfare, if so frisky a word as trotting can be used for those long vehicles, brightly parti-coloured under a canvas roof. Fat on the ground and low, they rolled glibly on old motor-tyres, and their horses also looked elongated like dachshunds, perhaps because of the harness, which seemed to be reins and a collar and very little else. Unlike the *droskys*, the buses kept an eye open for passengers, and had regular halts, and my favourite—which had 'Gül-Yolu' or 'Rose of the Road' written on a yellow background—used to stop by the door of the hotel. What one can do with a bus I never realized until, starting with my landlord's family for a party to the country one day, his wife pointed out to the driver that we were going farther than the rest of the passengers, and they all, kindly and with the greatest politeness, gave up their seats and walked.

My life in Antalya was changed by my acquaintance with this family. They lived on the far side of the terrace on which we all hung our washing or strolled in the evening to enjoy the sunset and the view; and when we came to know each other, the dreary masculine monopoly which saddens the Turkish world was at an end.

One could not imagine two more different sorts of life than those which the terrace divided. On my hotel side Avni wrestled with problems, from bills to the tap that died in one's hand, or the sanitation which unfortunately communicated with the wash-basins. Naji, who had been a country police-man, helped him. Very knowledgeable about forest roads, he was off-hand at dusting; though I could always tell when he had been by the cigarette-ends on my floor. In between these active spasms they relaxed, and some sad, drooping, taciturn friend was always ready to sit with them in silence at the draughty end of the stairs. But Avni was proud of his hotel, and of the bedrooms with two beds only and running water, and he spent his spirit cheerfully in a waste of ineffi-ciency—not his but other people's—doing the things that every sensible country would let its women do infinitely better.

The opposite side of the terrace, ruled by Avni's sister Muzaffer, was lapped in the easy Harim atmosphere of peace —a peace not quiet, but so secure that a surface ruffle of constant noise and chaos is essential to disguise the absolute stagnation of its pool. 'Women,' says Plutarch, 'if you take from them gold-embroidered shoes, bracelets, anklets, purple, and pearls, stay indoors.'[9] Deploring it in a rhetorical way, but queen of her secluded world, Muzaffer ran it with the additional security of her beauty. It was she who emptied the whole bus of its passengers with a turn of her voice. With a turreted crown on her head, she could have been one of those Tyches of the cities whom the later Greeks of the Aegean adored; her matronly stately plumpness and fresh complexion, her dark hair curling like hyacinth petals closely, the curve of nose and mouth, and white small teeth under soft lips that knew how to remain just rightly open in repose—all these assets Muzaffer knew and used discreetly, sitting with a little cup of coffee among those bullet-hard cushions of the Levant, receiving male relatives or female friends. What happened outside she neither knew nor cared for, since Muharrem her husband, who spent most of his leisure in his office, could obviously never be more happy and contented in his so-called working hours than in the more cheerful idleness of home.

But the two girls no longer belonged to this easy world, and were straining with all their generation against bars strong enough, in Antalya at any rate, to let the police stop the youngest on her bicycle, at the age of twelve, because such a sight was a disturbance in the street.

They were charming girls, full of cheerfulness and spirit. The elder was finishing her education in the north and taking an interest in fashions, while the younger, Seftab, advancing with graceful clumsiness through the borderlands of childhood, was still able—apart from bicycling—to move in freedom. She could play with her cousin, whom no doubt she might have been marrying later on if the old ways had not ended and progress were not lapping into the houses of Antalya year by year. On my latest visit, a man and a woman were strolling arm-in-arm on the esplanade in front of the hotel; the officers brought their wives to eat at the *lokanta*, and the younger ones came in bareheaded. All this was new. But Muzaffer kept to the older rules; and though she took her husband's arm in the discreet darkness of evening, she would first make herself respectable with a pair of tired stockings, and the ugly universal coat, and a kerchief knotted beneath the chin, until her regal presence achieved that defeated female air which makes the provincial city crowd of Turkey as depressing as a combustion engine with the spark removed.

6

MOUNT CLIMAX

*The Thracians had made him a road, the round journey being difficult and long.
He himself led his immediate followers along the coast, a route practicable only
with a north wind blowing; south winds make the passage along the shore
impossible.*

ARRIAN I, 26, 1.

IN EARLY SPRING THE BAY OF ANTALYA LIES UNDER A MIST
slightly raised above the surface of the water and filled with
sunlight, until the warmth of day sucks it up. I would
watch it from a slanting little breakfast shop that overhangs
the harbour. The six tiled domes of the Seljuk mosque, now
the museum, are there in the foreground with a minaret like
a bunch of asparagus beside them, rosy as if its bricks had been
scrubbed—which indeed they had been, by the Department of
Antiquities which has repaired them. Beyond these, brown
roofs and the tops of trees push out from hidden gardens; and
beyond them a caique might have been moving out from
Antalya with the dawn: she would leave a curved trail, marked
by the current, as wavering and edgeless as the seasonal pathways made by the feet of flocks; and beyond her and the misty
bay, the Chelidonian peninsula spread its tented blue festoons
from peak to peak. Every shade of azure was caught by
those pinnacles and in those valleys, and their height seemed
to vary with the hours, from its morning simplicity to the
magnificence of sunset, when only outlines showed and their
shadows were thrown across the sea. Or perhaps most
beautiful when the full moon hung over Cyprus invisible in the
south; then the foreground roofs became velvety and obscure
like scabious flowers, the walls and towers that remain were
arched over dark eclipses; and the far mountains rose into

73   G

Mount Climax

light as if the heavens above them opened and their earth were winged.

There, straight out of the west and well in sight, the pass led down from Lycia, where Alexander's army surmounted Mount Climax while he with his small escort rode through the shadowy borders by the sea. On my first visit to Antalya, I drove as far as I could to the west, along the sandy shore till the Karaman river stopped me, bridgeless, though shallow enough for a horse to ford if I had had one. I could do nothing about it and turned back, after looking at trees and islands, and the sheep-dipping that was being carried on in the sluggish stream.

But a few months later when I came with David Balfour in the *Elfin*, I asked him to put me ashore on that coast at Kemer. We made for a sandy cliff anchorage and walked inland through well-tilled plantations until, finding a prosperous village, we explained to the elders that a horse was required.

It was a busy time and the horses were mostly out in the

fields; and the village tailor, who had one, charged for the time he would have to waste over me and my journey, which made it expensive. Without consulting us, the elders rejected the tailor, another interval passed with glasses of tea and pauses, and at last a good-looking young man called Hasan was secured. Next morning, rather late, he reached the shore with a purple-tasselled, blue-beaded, cowrie-shell-decorated pony which he had waited to see shod in the village, as we asked him to do.

Our effort over this shoeing was a lesson in non-interference. Neither shoes nor stirrups were used by Greeks or Mace-donians,[1] and one is urged, somewhere in Xenophon, to walk one's horses about on stones to harden their feet. This is unnecessary in south-west Turkey, as the process takes place naturally whenever a horse walks about at all and the nomads, observed by Fellows, always rode them as they were. A few days before, my mount had lost three shoes out of four, and

I had walked for an hour or so and then got on again, having decided that he could suffer more easily than I could; but I had that remorse which we English keep chiefly for animals, and now insisted on the shoeing as a sort of atonement: and the poor pony, unused to it and cut too near his flesh, was already slightly lame as we left the village. The clouds too were threatening over Climax; and I set out with far more uncertainty than the troops of Alexander, whose steps had been cut and made easy for them by the top-knotted Thracian pioneers.[2]

After an hour's level riding we reached and forded the green Kemer river, about two feet deep in its bed of boulders against the steel-grey background of the gorge. Hasan, throwing me the rope by which my mild little animal was led, strode through without a thought for his moccasins and stockings, and for another hour we followed the stream, some hundred feet or more above it, between the rock-walls of Tahtali, the ancient Solyma, and Yeni Dagh. They sloped as if the sides of a funnel held us, and clouds hid their summits. There never can have been more than one way through the fierceness of the gorge, and the ledges my pony was clattering over might easily have been those of the Thracians, smoothed and polished to an alabaster whiteness with use and age.

Alexander had cut steps before to circumvent a mountain, when he opened the path over Ossa into Thessaly, and his rock shaped in the manner of a ladder is pointed out to this day. But the steel-grey Climax gorge is sterner than the vale of Tempe where the smooth Peneius flows.

The degrees of the mountain were hidden, so visible from the sea where they show as three horizontal bands, one above and behind the other, divided by black lines that are really more or less level shelves of pine and cedar. They climb in tiers to the watershed of Tahtali, and divide it both from Pisidia and the highlands of Termessus, and from the Lycian valley of the

Alağir Chay. No one visits their loneliness except the villagers of one hamlet and the people of the coast when they move to their summer pastures, nor did we meet a soul, but rode under clouds that drifted and dissolved and others came, as if the rock were spinning them as we spin words out of the very stuff we are made of, to vanish and melt in the stillness that produced them. The rock appeared and vanished, its furrows too steep for vegetation, while far below we looked on bright trees along the water—wild fig, myrtle, arbutus, laurel, cedar, olive, cornel, carob, sycamore and pine until—after an hour in the defile—the valley opened to a forest bowl where nothing but the river and the small noise of leaves that hid the valley floor were heard.

Here the Kemer comes from solitary sources, and we crossed it by a wooden bridge and left it, and zigzagged pleasantly in a northerly direction above a tributary valley. We rested for half an hour by water spouting into a hollow tree, and ate some pink *halva* that Hassan had bought in the village; then, still climbing the same hillside, came out upon the shelf from whose drop the gorge begins. Opposite and below us, was the hamlet of Kedialma in a patch of fields in the lap of the corrie, with a wall and square medieval tower among its little houses, an hour's ride away. The weather was too threatening to go there, for it would have kept us on the wrong side of the watershed for the night.

At about one in the afternoon, after reaching a second terrace scattered with oak trees, and signs of old shapeless cultivation, the high downs began to open, and we found a slope sown with corn and a few houses. In this *yaila*, called Ovajik, Hasan spends three months of summer, resting from his winter work which is the buying and selling of grain. We sat on the grass and drank yaourt and learned that Ovajik has been visited by Mr. Davis, who is spending his life over the Turkish flora and wandered here three years before. Otherwise, they told me, no one climbs up from Kemer, and my predecessors, Spratt and Forbes, are forgotten, who did the traverse in 1842.

They followed the ancient route between Lycia and Pamphylia by the ruins of Sarayjik[3] above the left bank of the Alağir Chay, and we must have crossed this point at about an hour's distance, seeing nothing, for from Ovajik onwards we climbed into mist. Pine trees loomed suddenly beside us, or a rough gate such as they use here—alone of all the eastern peoples I have known; it gave a familiar atmosphere, as of Dartmoor on a wet evening that darkens early, where I have so often ridden home over the drenched short turf that lies along the hill-tops, with all sight hidden and all sound smothered, yet the sense of direction safe in the horse's head. Such comfortable reliance was missing on these vague pasturelands of the Lycian border.

As we neared the watershed a thin drizzle turned into a deluge worthy of the sixty-one centimetre yearly rainfall of the plain. The whole hillside seemed to be slipping; the horse was lame and tired; the water poured through my burberry as if it were paper; and Hasan lost the way. It was essential to find the first habitations on the far slope before the fall of evening, and it was three o'clock already when we reached the top; but happily, before the end of another hour, we stepped out below the mists and saw a wet valley dark and clear below us, with patches of wheat round scattered homes. Wearily descending, we dismounted at the door of a house with broad eaves and a trellised verandah, and asked there for a lodging for the night.

The village was called Havazönü, and the house belonged to a well-to-do carpenter who was away with his wife in Antalya. His two sons and their sisters made us welcome, unsaddled the horse, swept out the upper room, lit a fire of pine-logs with the slice of a tree-trunk upright inside it, and dried my sodden clothes. It was my first evening in a Turkish village, and I remember it with gratitude as I now remember many others, all uniform in their kindness shown to strangers who happen to knock at any unknown door.

The windows had no glass, but were sheltered by criss-cross lattice work like the trellis of the verandah. All the woodwork of the house, the shutters, and cupboards, doors, the canopy of the hearth and the niches let into the wall which take the places of shelves or tables—all had been worked in simple fancy patterns of pine-wood by the carpenter or his sons. A mattress and bolsters to lean on were brought, and striped rugs of goat-wool such as is used for the making of tents; and after a while supper on a low table like a tray with legs, covered with a towel. Loaves of thin wheat were folded like napkins; eggs and beans cooked in fat, rice, milk, yaourt and honey were added, and coffee which is a luxury in the hills. Many of these people are fair; the sister, who never spoke, was beautiful, with straight eyebrows over grey eyes. The two young men, who ate with Hasan and me, were gay and easy, enjoying their remote life as a springboard for a world they hoped to see. One brother had gone off for six months as a sailor, and sent nylon shirts from the U.S.A., and printed cottons and a quilted coat for his sisters—things handled as the fine foreign garments Homer describes in the store-house at Ilium, laid away by Hecuba—the best ones at the bottom, in a chest in one corner of the room.

Even the children were fearless, and a little three-year-old tottered unprompted to kiss my hand. When supper was over, the men piled a few logs on the fire and left me; the tongues of the women were loosened and they pressed around me; and one of the more elderly, taking me by one hand with a lantern and spouted jug of water in the other, led me to a wooden hut in the yard where the sanitation was far better than that of the hotels in which I had suffered along the southern coast.

I had undressed and blown out my lamp (a thing the peasants never do) and was enjoying the firelight on guns and woollen saddle-bags hooked along the wall, restfully rejoicing at being no longer out with Alexander's army on the hillside in the rain, when the door opened and the elder woman came in. I shut my eyes, and she bent and tucked the quilt quietly round my shoulders, where a draught is apt to find one. With this last kindness in my mind I fell asleep.

Next morning the unknown valley shone like burnished metal from end to end, and mountain pyramids burned like the plumes of Sir Lancelot's helmet beyond its level rim in the blue sky. Tekeova Dagh as we rode showed a triangle of rock behind us in the south, and a snow-streak of Solyma appeared and was hidden. The fortress of Beydagh and Bakirli held the west, with patches of snow across the Alağir watershed; and in the north Chalbali or Bereket (the two names seemed to be used indifferently) was the companion of our day. Like a high wave sucking at our valley it stood across the Chandir river, and rose fold upon fold to tired and snow-worn stones.

Patches of corn were scattered on the uneven ledges like laundry in the sun. The landscape was open, as the great mountain valleys are, where travel moves across from one end to the other, and the slopes hold curves of all sorts for the lodging of villages and fields. The houses, mostly hidden in trees, were old-fashioned, copied by the Lycians in their tombs two thousand years ago. The only tombs I saw, however, were Muslim and late, built with four wooden planks and sometimes a carved turban, and the only sarcophagi known are those seen by Spratt, Daniell and the Austrian Schönborn, near the Genoese fortress two hours from Chandir village, where the upper and lower levels of the valley are separated by a defile, and a medieval castle holds the pass.

I was not yet at this time aware of a problem in the geography of Alexander's marches, nor had I read the accounts of the two former journeys down this valley, or I would have ridden down to the castle instead of merely looking at it through my glasses from our high path on the hill. For somewhere in this region was the Pisidian fort whose capture from Phaselis is mentioned by Arrian and given by Diodorus in full;[4] and the acropolis of Sarayjik and the ruins above Chandir have both been selected, by travellers, as the likely site.* That it was on or near the route from Lycia to Pamphylia is generally agreed, and Arrian makes it clear that it was in the territory of Phaselis, for he says that the Pisidians 'injured those of Phaselis who were tilling the ground'. I believe on the whole, with Schönborn and Daniell, that the Chandir valley fortress is the more likely place, and have given my reasons at the end of this book in the appendix on Alexander's marches. But this preference is very tentative, based only on a general view of the positions and the greater accessibility of the Chandir valley to the marauding Pisidians on their heights; and I think with regret of how easily I could have spent two more days and satisfied myself with a closer view, if my knowledge had been more adequate at the time.

Our track turned north-eastward through glades and forests. With many ups and downs and dips into tributary valleys, it gradually descended. Sometimes it was steep, or barely scooped out of a cliff-side; sometimes it lay easily for long stretches where the Turks have planned a new road along the ancient way; and for hours together it led under the cone-spotted ceiling of the pines. It kept high on the right of the valley, passing Armutjuk, Chinarak, Akjaisa—hamlets so scattered that only stray houses were noticeable among the trees; and beyond the last of these we watched the Chandir river far below slip down into its gorge and disappear. Two clefts or ravines come in here from either side to where the gorge breaks and the castle with round towers holds the valley,

* For Alexander's routes see maps in Appendix I.

and it is here—'on the left bank of Tchandir by the Genoese fortress two hours from Tchandir village'[5]—that Daniell conceived the fortress taken by the Macedonians to have stood. It is not impossible that the old route may have threaded the left bank of the river; there are a few ruins on a crag north of the stream just below Havazönü, and no signs of anything ancient on the right bank where I rode, though the directness of this route and the ease of its watershed from Alagir to Chandir are all in its favour. Right or left, the Lycian highroad to Pamphylia must have run down the valley, since there is no other way: and the Pisidian stronghold must have been near enough to threaten it, since this was the only good reason for the robbers to want it, or for Alexander to think it worth the trouble of a siege. As we rode, the Pamphylian plain and sandy shore gradually opened before us, at the end of a long avenue of lessening hills.

Most of the hours went by in solitude, in the woods where Spratt said that bears 'abounded', though not a shadow of one was to be seen. Whenever we found a thread of water, spouting brown into a hollow tree, Hasan would fill my cup and bring it, with one hand on his breast, and we rested; and, if anyone came by, I would try to extract the names of the localities, which was difficult, since the valley itself changed its name with every stretch of its river, and no one was interested in more than a mile or two of its course. Our only trouble was the pony, that now had gone badly lame.

"He will get accustomed, he will get accustomed," said Hasan, walking steadily ahead like a Nanny who will not listen, until I distressed him by walking. He bore this for some time, and then collected a man with a mule from a field below the forest, and I rode in discomfort to please him, and then disappointed him by walking again. The plain was now near. Sinuous ridges like lizards melted into it; on the left, our valley rose towards the highlands of Termessus, whose shepherds must have watched the glitter of the Macedonian spears. Their hills broke to the isolated rocks of Sivri Dagh, while Gedelle and a black Matterhorn crystal called Kara Dagh divided us from goat-paths on our right that led into the heights of Climax. We came out by the Gök Derè and an hour's flat going, along river-bed oleanders and by Yürük camps, to the Sarichinar river flowing stagnant in the plain with the sunset behind it. An old Turkish bridge crossed it, and an easy road led to the Karaman whose banks I had reached from Antalya. There, in a modern farm on the western side, they telephoned for a taxi and ferried me across to it in a tractor: we had been eight hours, and two more resting, on our way—fifteen hours of actual walking or riding in the two days from Kemer over Climax. This was considered fast going, and Hasan indeed was an excellent tough young man of twenty-five. The pony, though it stood abjectly with one foot bent and its underlip hanging, still managed, to my relief, to whinny to a mare when it saw one; and would be no worse off than we all are after a heavy day when our turn comes.

*   *   *   *

My next visit to Climax was in 1956 from Antalya.

Bairam was then beginning. Among the calls of the muezzin at their appointed hours the end of Ramadhan was announced with blasts of sirens. Electric lights sprang up round minarets in a primrose dusk where swifts, or perhaps swallows, were darting. And a vague buzz of pleasure filled the air.

I walked about my terrace quietly contented, as if the world and I belonged to each other far from all personal tensions—the feeling of a haven; and as I watched the swallows I thought of my private unhappiness, so long ago—nearly forty years—how deep it had been, and how it had healed, and all had turned to life; as if, in the agony of one's heart, one were kneaded into a substance subtle enough to melt into existence, and could see one's own soul, and everyone's for that matter, stepping out small and brave under the tall illuminated archway of its past.

Seftab, coming on to the terrace, kissed her hand to the thin crescent of the moon. "The Prophet's eyebrow," she said,

> "I saw Allah
> I believed in Allah
> Light to my face
> Health to my eyes: ah, ha,"

she added, and explained that one greets the new moon with a laugh.

It was hanging above Climax whose steps appeared south of the Lycian pass and against the shadows of the farther hills. The promontories all showed clearly against it, Kemer and Phoenix and the far Chelidonian home of the eagles where the sea and sky were meeting.

"When are you going to take me to look at Alexander's road round the bay?" I asked.

"Soon," said Seftab. "When my father has mended the motor-boat."

Weeks passed; but eventually, just before I was leaving, Muharrem sat up a whole night and announced that the boat was mended and we would leave at six. Muzaffer packed samovar and picnic; Avni took a day from the dark desk near the stair; and with the girls and two young helpers and myself, we pushed out from harbour under the bows of an American destroyer. The morning lay quiet on the water, and nothing but our own furrow, curled like a white feather, followed us across the bay.

In an hour we had reached the Karaman estuary, and saw buildings put up by N.A.T.O. beyond a sandy curve not far from ancient Olbia, where people come to bathe from huts of reeds. On our right we left the Lycian pass; we left, too, the unknown sites of Thebe and Lyrnessus. The coast grew steep and lovely, and we followed it southward to where the slopes of Climax dip to the sea.

Mr. Daniell, a traveller some hundred years ago, had ridden here below them, and found the way flat except for a craggy portion in the south; and we could see how he went, skirting the sandy bays and climbing low ridges, where the built-up stones of an old track were visible here and there. On the heights above, straggling bush thinned to single trees and ended in walls of rock slung from ravine to ravine like garlands. As I had already been told, there is only one way to the heights of Climax on this side, apart from the Kemer gorge, and that is called Göynük, and it enters a cleft south of the hamlet of Beldibi, the solitary inhabited spot on all this stretch of rock and sea.

The Göynük path is scarcely used, they told me, and would obviously have been longer than the Kemer gorge for Alexander's army. His own way, in the water, stood in sight. Chaltijik is the more northerly and the higher of two promontories, a naked face of pink rock where a new tourist road, chipping hopefully to the middle of a precipice, gives up the struggle and dies in mid-air. An anchorage is marked where the northern edge meets sandy stretches of a shallow bay and traces of the road are seen; and the truth about the southerly gales and their violence is shown by the rusty skeleton of a small ship, lifted high across the beach and thrown among the trees. The ancient road here might be flooded by a southerly sea on its sandy stretches; but the rocky promontory could never be an obstacle, since an easy neck leads across it, a very short distance inland; the beach too is shallow at its foot even today. The more southerly cliff, whose name is not thought worth a mention either by Beaufort or the Mediterranean Pilot, is more likely to have been the crucial passage, since the sea washes around it more deeply and the detour is far longer at its back.

It was this that we were making for, and its name—Muharrem told me—was the Headland of Drops, Damlajik Burnu. "We will picnic there," said he, pointing to a strip of white gravel against a shadeless face of rock. A fringe of pine trees bent over the edge above and showed the steepness of the hidden slope ascending; and fallen boulders lay strewn about, polished to a satin smoothness by the waves. On this unpromising spot we landed in water clear as daylight, on a beach of small bright gravel; and saw, a few steps away, the opening of a cave. The precipice slanted across it, leaving an easy height of a man for an entrance; and a lofty natural room opened inside, cool in a pale green twilight, with a white-and-pink floor and a clean smell of the sea. A high canopy at the inner end was damp with moss and little pools, dripping on to stalagmites with a noise of drops that fell in twos and threes in different places, but never in a stream. The water was sweet, and hornets, plum-coloured with yellow bars, came here to drink it, sailing round the precipice, clustering their angular legs on the moss, folding back their polished leaf-veined wings, and sailing out again across the sunlit band of shore and sea. Here we lit a fire and filled the samovar, cut bread and cucumbers and tomatoes, and laid out the salt on the stones; and we slept in the fresh airy solitude, under the pleasant smoke-smell of the fire. Ender, with pretty bare feet, plump fingers, and tiny waist—all the ingredients of mythology about her—stood pouring out our tea. Beyond the moist and cool glitter of the drops around us nothing was in sight except a dazzling horizon, and a far curve of the distant Taurus. At any moment, I thought, as I lay with my eyes half-closed, the young Macedonian captains might come riding round the precipice, waist-high in water, delighted with the veering north wind that leaves the beaches free.

Ender and I swam round the tip of the headland. The water dropped beyond our depth, or that of any horseman, for boulders have rolled from the overhanging rock and the way round has probably been pushed farther out to sea than it was before.

This circumventing of Climax was in any case no very memorable feat, nor did Alexander pride himself upon it; the short cut does no more than save a few hours of up and down going, by the inland way which Mr. Daniell followed in 1842 and which must in some form have existed when Phaselis was a flourishing city. The people of Kemer or Tekirova use it today, when they are unable to cross their bay by sea and are forced to a twelve or fifteen hours' ride. Their track, which is shown on the modern map, climbs behind the two promontories and runs along the coast again south of Beldibi. 'With the exception of a few hours' ride over an excessively rocky and craggy road' it 'passes over plain'; and it was the rocky bit that Alexander rode into the ocean to avoid.

A waveless sea lay in the bays and inlets as we chugged home in the afternoon. The shallow green water showed the iridescent sand beneath it, and the road could be seen clearly built where it rose from the beaches, with square stones that belonged to a day when more important places than the present were spaced along this coast. It is still known as the Unbelievers' Way—a reference probably to the Genoese, or such people as inhabited the islet of Rashat which—with medieval ruins and olives gone to wildness—lifts its miniature precipice under the lee of the land.

An afternoon breeze was raising small choppy ridges before the bay was crossed. They moved in solid wedges, unrecognizable as the transparent morning water we had left round Alexander's footsteps near the cave. The upper bungalows of Antalya on the cliffs drew nearer, and we slipped again under the bows of the American destroyer, where a sailor was strolling in the sun. He looked down with kind nonchalance from his height, with all his wealth and one hundred and thirty million fellow-citizens behind him; and it is very unlikely that he knew how all in his own civilization that really matters had been carried here before him, by a lad with seventy talents and a few companions, riding their little ponies round the bay.

7

THE PAMPHYLIAN DEFILES

Alexander moved to Perge and thence began his march to Phrygia, which led past Termessus . . . A height runs from the city to the road and there ends; but opposite is a height equally abrupt. These make natural gates . . . and a small guard can cut off all approach. Alexander passed the narrow passage and encamped near the city.

ARRIAN I, 27, 5–8.

THE SPRING WAS ALREADY PUSHING INTO SUMMER. CHERRIES and apricots and syrupy sweet mulberries in baskets appeared; the first warm day in May had reached the plain, though a light coat was still useful.

People began to sit outside the doorsteps of their shops in the High Street of Antalya, where a sad little pastime could be indulged in with a scraggy rooster perched on a sky-blue box with screws of paper before him: for five *kurush* he pulled one out, crowed, flapped his wings at a white rabbit beside him, and offered you your fortune.

The *lokanta* laid tables on a terrace roof and one could dine with the outline of Antalya below, watching it turn from nectarine to brown, while the rose-coloured minaret gathered the remaining light, and even the new bungalows on the cliff began to mellow, set in square gardens full of flowers.

Ender and I bathed on the western *plage*, hiring a *drosky* whose horses, when they reached the steepness of the hill, had learned to rid themselves of frightened passengers by biting each other's necks. Or we drove in the other direction, to where the cliffs sink, and the shapeless brick ruins at La'ara were covered with a magenta carpet of blossoming thyme. Straw huts were going up here and painted chairs collecting round an old church now turned into a 'gazino'. Scabious and

89   H

hollyhocks were everywhere in flower, and the waterfalls of
Catarrhactes showed full and white over their cliffs.   Solyma
too was white in the west, though on the southern slopes of
Taurus the snow had melted; and pink powder-puffs of cloud
floated through the sunsets, in the cold northerly stream of the
upper air.

In the evening light the mountains, jutting from their valleys,
looked flat and thin like theatre wings.   Their uneven line
broke behind Perge to an open horizon—and another wide
gap appeared north of Antalya.   It was the sight of this apparent easiness, compared with the rugged sunset bastions of
Termessus, that made me wonder what induced Alexander to
make west from Pamphylia; for going, according to Arrian,
from Perge to Phrygia in the north, 'his march led past Termessus'.   Why?

I had climbed up to that city with two Czechs on my first
visit to Antalya.   After a casual lift on the Perge road, we
drove together next day to the café at Güllük, which then stood
alone in the landscape.   A spring was splashing into a sarcophagus by a shed of scattered tables, and drivers to the plateau
stopped for a glass of tea.   From here a shepherd boy led us for
two hours along a path that slants through woods, to where the
town is slung like a hammock between sharp ridges.

The trees, already leafy down below, were jewelled and transparent here with buds; ash, oak, bay and cherry in flower,
daphne and arbutus among them—they wove themselves so
thickly that we scarcely noticed the city gate speckled with
patterns of branches as we stepped through.   Out of Pisidian
roughness and tribal foundations easily Hellenized, Termessus
emerged and flourished with many temples.   Their doors and
pediments and tumbled columns survive in the descending
basins of the valley; and the pedestals of stoas show Greek
inscriptions, where lichens and spring shadows blur the forgotten names.   A great wall, six feet wide or more, still stands

across the inner valley, with the disc carved upon it which seems to be the sign of Termessus, so frequent is it on all the tombs that scatter the crests of the enclosing hills. Beyond it, the street led to temples, a grass-grown market, a gymnasium shadowed by budding plane trees like an Oxford quad in spring; and at last, on the tip of the defile, to the most beautifully sited of all Pamphylian theatres, whose shallow stone seats and enfolding crags look three thousand feet down a straight ravine to the sea.

The shepherd led on under oak trees, among stone sarcophagi shaken together by earthquakes as if at any moment their Dantesque lids might move under the steps of sinners; until the oak gave way to pine and the hillside opened, and there appeared the rough snow of Tahtali Dagh and the smooth snow of the flattening plateau highlands.

Her children must have loved a city so high, so strong, so beautiful and remote, whether they greeted her climbing from the hollow valley as we had done, or by the path from the head of the defile, that runs to the eastern and the oldest wall. On the long ridges north and south, the precipice itself is the only fortification, and tombs and cisterns are peacefully chiselled into the few and difficult honeycomb crannies of the rock.

No Christian church or cathedral, as in the other cities, seems to have stood in Termessus where once its temples stood.[1] It emerged into history with a short robust record in the wars of Alexander and his successors, settled a colony in Cibyritis,[2] bribed Manlius in 189 B.C. with fifty talents, left an inscription among its monuments to Plato and the Muses, and faded back into its mountain solitude until Dr. Clarke rediscovered it about a hundred and twenty years ago.[3]

In the generation that followed Alexander it left a tragic story. Alcetas, one of his officers, commander of a battalion of the Phalanx in Bactria and brother of Perdiccas, was sent after the king's death to western Pisidia, and built up a strong friendship with the mountaineers. When Perdiccas was murdered, and his generals defeated by Antigonus and Alcetas himself put to flight, he escaped with six thousand Pisidians to Termessus, and the young men of the city fought for him against Antigonus' forty thousand men and refused to give him up. Their more prudent parents and elders betrayed him, choosing a moment when the young warriors were away; and Alcetas 'laid hands on himself not to come into the power of his enemies' and his dead body was wrapped in a cloak and carried to Antigonus among the rocks. Maltreated and exposed the young men recovered it when Antigonus departed, and buried it honourably as Diodorus tells.[4]

I repeated this story to the Czech professor and his wife, who were enjoying the peace and beauty of the spring in the tameless city. To them, tossed through concentration camps in Europe, with only each other to hold on to in their battered world—with their very name, Heribert Grubitch, reminiscent of forgotten invasions—the sorrows of Termessus were a part of everyday history, and the climax of the centuries was this quiet oasis of a day. It was touching to see them among the columns, the standing lintels and fallen pedestals, enjoying the thinly-veiled velvety solitude of the valley. Under the opening leaves the lattice-shadows touched tree-trunks and stone with light fingers, as fugitive and swift as the glitter and the darkness that a current swallows at the bend of a stream.

A Yürük with his family had pitched two small tents in the lowest lap of the city. They lived there with their goats and dogs around them, and they had dragged temple columns end on end to shore up a brooklet that watered their grazing. The old man sat, unwelcoming, to watch us, from a heap of the temple stones where two draped marble figures vaguely showed.

He too, like the ancient Termessians, had no wish to see his privacy invaded, and, as he was also deaf, it took some time for the shepherd guide to get the matter of the country we belonged to settled—the most important point about a stranger in the eyes of every Turkish peasant I have met. "Pek Güzel, very good," they usually say when one is English; and ask some rather surprising constitutional question, such as whether a two-party government is good?

"And should the opposition take its turn?"

"Yes," I say, "if you have two horses and one carriage, it is better for each of them to pull."

But the Termessian in his old fashion had been brought up to think of strangers as infidels. He allowed his dogs to growl while he sat with hands gnarled on the crook of his stick, and a daughter with two children at her skirts stood smiling in silence. When we came down again, some four hours later, they were away, looking after their goats and kids among the arbutus. We were tired, and so was our young guide, trailing a sapling for firewood from his shoulder along the stony path; and we were glad to rest at the wayside café at the bottom of the hill.

The road lies in a hollow valley below the northern face of the Termessus mountain and climbs gradually to a pass at its north-western end. It is the main road to Korkuteli (Isinda) and runs along or near its ancient predecessor. The two diverge when the height of the pass is reached. The modern road takes a wide and beautiful bend to the southerly outskirts of the defile; there it looks over wooded hills to the levels and summits of the Beydagh range and all the Termessian high-lands, until it winds back between narrow sides under watch-towers that the old road has been following all along: and the old road, unfit now for cars, dusty among stones flattened by herds and flocks of many generations, has a branch at what is called on the map Injirji Kahvesi or the Place-of-Figs'-café that leads to Bademağachi, the ancient Ariassus, and through the Pisidian country to Phrygia. Alexander either followed this route or otherwise retraced his steps for five miles or so from the entrance of the Termessus valley, and marched north, more directly, by what later became the main south and north road from Antalya, over the steep but short Dösheme pass.

I looked at both these routes and it is obvious, from the fact of his attack on Termessus, that either the Isinda or the Bademağachi road were in Alexander's mind to begin with. His change and turn to the north against Sagalassus may have been suggested by the Selgians, who arrived at the Macedonian camp just after Termessus had been beaten in a night attack in the valley. A later, Hellenistic wall, with a gate and a rampart of ten towers, is slung across from hill to hill in the position indicated by Arrian as that of the Termessus defence.*⁵ The towers and their doors, however, face so as to show that the fortification was intended against, and not for, the people of Termessus on their hill. The building is of the 2nd century B.C. and probably belongs to someone—Attalus of Pergamum perhaps—who remembered or feared the menace of the Pisidians.

The position, anyway, at the valley's eastern end, gives the choice of two routes for Alexander's onward march. He either continued under the long cliff and the western defences of unconquered Termessus, half-way up the long defile to the Bademağachi track; or he may, after the Selgians had given their advice, have changed his route as completely as he changed his plan, and—leaving Termessus alone since it had become unimportant—retraced his steps some five miles or so into the plain of Pamphylia and marched north to the plateau by Kirkgöz and Dösheme.

---

* The Loeb translation is misleading as it suggests that the defence position ran *up* from the city: but the Greek text (kindly translated for me by Sir Harry Luke, K.C.M.G. and Mr. David Balfour) does not imply this, and the actual fact is that the two hills slope *down* to the road from either side.

Although I had no time to follow them in all their length, I looked at both ends of both these routes and walked for some way along them. In the north, they break out, not far one from the other, on either side of the modern main road along the flat plateau to Burdur, which follows a third and middle way between them through the defiles of the hills. Old men remember the making of this new road some sixty or seventy years ago. The earlier track can still be followed. It winds down the Termessus valley in an easterly direction through the gate of the wall, joins the new road under glades of pines, and breaks away again to run through cornfields and under stunted olives round the north-east mountain entrance of the valley, from under whose hill a smoothly-jointed Hellenistic guard tower watches the flat lands beyond.

The bed of the Kuru Chay, dry as its name suggests, also comes down here from the Termessus valley. It circumvents both the hill and the wall, which adds to its other disappointments by not crossing the river or indeed closing the valley at all. Descending from the Termessus hill, it swings up the small opposing slope in a reasonable way, and then dies like the Maginot line in mid-air: the little hill is an isolated outcrop, and any sensible army would circumvent it by following the bed of the Kuru Chay behind it; and this seems to me to be the only inaccuracy in Arrian's description, which declares that 'a small guard can cut off all approach'.

Farther down, and also on the north of the Kuru Chay, but in flat pinelands that turn to cultivation, was a city whose water-channels adorned with altars I have already mentioned. It looks like a late town, and Spratt identified it with Lagon. Since my map placed it to the south of the road instead of to the north, it took me some time to find. These absent-minded moments in the cartographer's head cause a lot of trouble. But the taxi-driver and I finally located it at the Café of the Far, or Long, Well (Uzunkuyu Kahvesi), seventeen kilometres from Antalya, now grown from a village of fifteen to one of seventy-five houses, to the damage of its ruins.

If I were rich, I should like to restore the little town of Lagon. It must have prospered on the traffic of the road which, for centuries before the old men remember, ran northward along the western edge of the plain. The water, too, in its straight channels, must have kept Lagon happy, and paid for its street of columns now prostrate, and for the temple heaped at its centre. Four long strips or more of carved cornice, pillars diagonally fluted, fragments of a coffered ceiling and winged naked figures with garlands, all lie together, so that it would be no very great labour to set them up where they stood. How pleasant for the people of Antalya in summer, when they come, as they do, to picnic in the pine-woods, to see their ancient city blossoming like a bed of lilies on its columns. Its waters are reviving, and the peasants have cleared the former channels, that run along stone blocks, about three feet high, where the water has left an overlapping incrustation of lime. The peasants use it and dig new gardens, and every turn of the spade uncovers some bit of stone or marble, Byzantine or Roman, mostly doomed to disappear.

A line of caravanserais or *hans* was built in Seljuk times along this road. The finest of them is at the top of Dösheme, on the plateau, at a village called Susuz, the Waterless, east of the modern main road and north of Melliköy. Nineteenth-century travellers rode by its door and noticed floating figures in stiff relief, and thought them angels; and the inside of the *han* has an unusual cathedral quality, with a domed nave, and arches on piers rising from it, where the cattle now enter a Rembrandt gloom under the stalactite carving of the door. Some part of the front wall must have belonged to an older building, but the rest of it—with slit windows widening inward, and buttresses, round, square, octagonal and hexagonal, four on each side—is Seljuk at its best.

The other two *hans* are in the plain, one at Kirkgöz and one at the cross-roads at Lagon. They also have fine doors of a simpler pattern; and they open to double arcades on an enclosed court, where Spratt and his party lit their fires and picketed their horses as travellers did through the ages, lodging together with their pack-animals in the outer and inner rooms. These *hans* too have buttressed walls, square, squat and windowless, fortified to suit the commerce of their day. The traffic of the Crusades came by as well as the earlier trading; the Byzantine heritage is shown at Kirkgöz by charming shallow domes of overlapping tiles; and, fold within fold of civilization, my eye fell upon a small altar with a Greek inscription, let into the Seljuk building of the wall.

Kirkgöz must always have had a road because of the water that gushes out here between the hillside and the plain. Lorry-drivers today stop and sleep in the shade through the hot hours before continuing their journey, as their predecessors did before them; and tables with napkins and glasses are laid under plane trees beside a water-lily lake in sight of the Seljuk *han*. The road divides, and the middle modern way turns up into the hills; while the old leads to Dösheme, a few miles farther north.

I turned off the main road at Mellik̈oy to examine the top of this pass, by two small rises with fragmentary ruins and a report of further antiquities at Chakraz, on the left. These seemed to be high up and far away in the hills, and—refusing to be led astray—I made for the plateau's edge, as far as the taxi could go. There the Dösheme track tilted steeply downward towards the peacock colours of the plain, and after walking half an hour or so, I was about to dismiss the pass for its steepness when some ancient wheel-ruts caught my eye. They continued on and off about three feet above the present level of the path, which had evidently washed away between them; and they had worn deep wide grooves in the limestone, over a long period of time. Delighted with this evidence, and thinking how agonizing the jolting must have been before springs or rubber tyres were invented, I made as soon as I could for the other end of the pass, beyond Kirkgöz, in the plain.

Each one of these investigations meant a separate expedition from Antalya in a taxi, since the places that buses went to were nearly always far away from ruins. My driver had become trained to deal with ditch or stubble; and this was necessary for the finding of Dösheme which, forty-one kilometres from Antalya, is now scarcely used. The cart-tracks that lead from village to village in the plain had given out before we saw the old route creeping, with shallow undulations like an asp between the breasts of low steep hills. Walls of large but mean buildings showed its importance in the time of the Byzantines and Crusaders; and it continued to be used, and to be referred to by the name of Bijikli village, by the 19th-century travellers. The many towers, cornices and columns seen by Koehler[6] have disappeared, but stretches of original wall are still there under medieval building, and sarcophagi, carved with rosettes, Greek inscriptions, shields, convoluted angles, and even a mutilated sprawling lion, are scattered about, too heavy to carry away from the base of the hill. They flank a causeway whose pavement is eight or nine feet across, edged with big stones, evidently built in an age of Christian vandalism, since lids of tombs have been used here and there in its surface. Ruts are deeply worn in the stones, and these must themselves have been preceded by a more ancient road, built perhaps by Attalus when he founded his port of Attaleia, when the sarcophagi stood to right and left on the hillside before another age broke them to bits.

I climbed for nearly an hour, and sat down to rest and look back over the sun-drenched plain, where the reaped stems lay in rows and caught the sunlight among the standing corn. Grassy avenues had been left for village carts and tractors to move among their harvests.

The plain curved north-eastward; hills floated into it like grey swans into a lake whose northern shore was the great gap of Perge. It looked as if the easiest of all the passes must be there, and indeed somewhere in that direction is the opening which Augustus later fortified with a garrison at Cremna.[7] Alexander would never have turned away to Termessus if his intention had been to make north! Of so much I felt certain though the reason was still obscure. He meant to go towards the west when he started from Perge. The Selgian ambassadors or some other information turned him to the lands of Sagalassus in the north, and he either made for them by this way, or else marched by Termessus as he had marched under the walls of Sillyon, and came out near Ariassus on to the upper plain.

Ariassus was easy to find at Bademağachi, a friendly village of prosperous houses scattered west of the main road, fifty-six kilometres from Antalya, among fruit trees on warm slopes. All these passes are free of heavy snows in spite of their rise to the plateau, and this no doubt the envoys from Phaselis stressed when they urged Alexander to abandon the high frozen uplands of Xanthus.

In Bademağachi, the Almond-Tree village, we drank our glasses of tea in the shade of the square, and walked with a schoolmaster for the inside of an hour over the ups and downs of a low promontory sown with corn, to where the ruins slide down the slope of a narrow valley, and a Roman triple gate of the age of Hadrian stands neat and slender at their foot. Beyond it the cultivated plateau shows to the rims of the Sagalassus hills. The position dominates both the modern road and that of the Termessus defile, one on either side; and the importance of the place is shown by the span of its ruins, that cover the hill. The huge blocks of a heraion were beside us, a high tomb with a double alcove beyond it, and the fallen pillars of a church near-by.

Most of this, except the heraion, seemed late; there was a slickness about it, as if the architect, after too much building, no longer respected each work separately for itself, but copied merely. That is decadence, I thought, as I wandered among the thorns—in architecture, in life, and in literature also. As the architect his stone, so the writer too keeps his idea side by side in his mind with the sentences that describe it, to see them continually together, so that reality may rule his words, in a human proportion, and the fact and its reporting may not deviate one from the other and truth be lost. Decadence is their divergence, a gap between the conception and its expression, a slackening of the discipline that unites us with vision: and excellence, which alone matters in a world that neglects it, lies almost entirely in this coincidence of the thing with its expression. However humble or unimportant the object may be, this is true, and even the bows and ribbons of la Pompadour are remembered because they were *right*.

But who cares for what happened in Ariassus, when Alexander had passed? The provincials went on building their sepulchres, one like the other, and are forgotten, while his torch moves down the solitary valley. The inert walls and ruined tombs and empty churches glow for a moment in their obscure and thorny thickets. The pride which made them comfortable and rich has long departed and among their dead stones nothing but a young man's dream remains. But as I came away, the Dösheme pass still seemed to me the most likely for Alexander's passage since it did not have an unconquered enemy on the defile behind it. However this may be, from one road or the other, he marched across the plateau to Sagalassus at the spring turn of the year, across lands that lie like pools between sudden ranges, where men walk on the winter-flattened pastures with their flocks behind them as soon as the March snow melts.

Sagalassus

Ağlason, the modern village, leans in gardens against a mountain that spills waters down wooden shoots for mills. Pieces of marble, lintel, cornice, or column are put to poor villages uses, as familiar and unrecognized as the civilization they brought and belonged to; and in the square, under a tree, with the new school behind it, the countrymen have stood a statue from the city above. With its name slightly altered, Ağlason—Sagalassus, Shakalsha of the Egyptians[8]—it is on a shoulder of the mountain, as straight as one can go.

The ascent is so steep that the sight of the shelf and all its ruined buildings is long hidden. A road cuts through it, leading to Isparta, but in the chaos of rocks, ravines and tangled ranges, one would scarcely notice that the grey lichened stones on either hand were once a carved and decorated town, if it were not for the theatre, oriented to a church and shaken by earthquakes, and backed by funeral niches on the vast face of the cliff. The outlines of a main street run southward on a spur, and many temples with pieces of sculpture still about them show the strength and grandeur of this 'fairly large city' of the most warlike of the warlike Pisidians.

A shepherdess, knitting a sock, showed us the metopes and fallen sculptures that she knew. And when we had spent some hours here, on our way as we descended, we saw a little car and two figures rather lost beside it—a husband and wife who had driven from Paris without a word of anything but French, and were looking for Sagalassus unnoticed beside them in the vast landscape. Below it in the plain, the spring had come; we looked down on cultivated hollows like spoons among the hills where the shallow lakes of winter were drying; there the poplars shimmered as if with sequins on silver, the walnuts curled infant leaves bright and brown as polished leather, the pear trees were thick and tight with blossom like Victorian nosegays in every sheltered hollow. People were out, riding or walking near the villages; the manes and tails of grazing horses were ruffled in the breeze; women were weeding, kneeling in rows; or hoeing, one behind the other, with a man at ease to direct them; and oxen were ploughing, four or five teams together. All were in groups, spaced here and there like a ballet of the works of spring.

The buffaloes were being taken along the plain in droves, with some old plough, shiny with handling, askew on a donkey among them; and our zigzag road and the short cuts of the steep hill beneath us were being climbed in long files to the earliest mountain pastures by young creatures out for the first time—kids and calves, white lambs with black ears, small girls dressed like their mothers, in quilted jackets and full trousers that turn the female body into an egg-shaped oval below the breasts. They looked free and sweet. So did their brothers, in rags surmounted by new peaked caps bought at the fair or *bairam* in Ağlason below.

At the foot of the hill, with the same spring air about him, and without his cuirass, for he rarely wore it in battle, Alexander too was marshalling his army, if one had eyes to see.

He was fighting to reach his base and reinforcements in the north, and the battle is described by Arrian with great care—the marshalling of the phalanx at the foot of the slope, from Alexander with his bodyguard on the right to the territorial foot 'in touch with them, up to the left wing, all under the battalion officers in the order of precedence for the day'. On the right wing in advance were the archers and the Agrianes light-armed from the upper Struma; on the left the Thracian javelin men; and no cavalry, for they would have been useless on the steepness of the hill.*

---

* The Loeb translation declares the battlefield to have been unsuitable for cavalry because *narrow*. This is incorrect, as the hillside is wide and open, but rough and steep, and *difficult* rather than narrow is a correct translation, or 'rough and unfavourable' as given by E. J. Chinnock in 1893. (Arrian I, 28, 4). See Curtius, IV, 13, 25, for Alexander's cuirass: it would not be worn up so steep a hill.

The forcing of the Defiles

The Pisidians, and the Termessians who had joined them, 'occupied the hill in front of the city which was as strong for defensive operations as the wall itself, and held their ground'. The walled city and the cliff that rises from it were behind them, and already Alexander's right wing was advancing. It was climbing the steep part of the ascent, where the Pisidians attacked from ambuscades among the boulders on either hand; and the archers were driven back; but the Agrianes held. 'The Macedonian phalanx was coming up, and Alexander himself was visible at its head': and the battle became hand to hand, the unarmoured mountaineers charging the overlapping shields and^9 long advancing spears. Some five hundred lay dead, and the rest knew their way and fled among the rocks, while the Macedonians, 'from weight of armour and want of local knowledge, had little heart for the pursuit'. They were out of breath no doubt, but Alexander kept on the heels of the flyers and stormed the city, and 'then he attacked the remaining Pisidians, capturing many of their forts'. He marched on, by Lake Ascania or Burdur, regions where waters flow naked through sandy landscapes, and villages are screened in poplars, and few tracks wind among stones; to Celaenae, now Dinar, and on to Gordium, where the forces that led to Issus were waiting.

8

SELGE

At this point arrived envoys from the Selgians, who are also native Pisidians with a large city, a warlike people; they had been for some time at enmity with the Termessians and so had sent an embassy to Alexander to ask for his friendship. Alexander granted their wish, and found them wholly trustworthy allies.

ARRIAN I, 28, I.

THERE IS NOTHING EXPLICIT IN ARRIAN TO LINK THE SELGIANS with Alexander's change of plan; but the fact is clear that he did change it, turning from the west to the Sagalassians in the north, who were the enemies of the Selgians. They were at any rate the close allies of the Selgians' enemies, and Alexander did this immediately after meeting the Selgian ambassadors under the gates of Termessus. It is therefore possible that their being singled out as 'trustworthy allies' may refer to the important information they gave, and the opening of the defiles which followed. Other advisers, from Phaselis or Perge, had encouraged Alexander to destroy the Termessians on their own borders rather than the distant Sagalassians; and the Selgians, pointing out an easier and a shorter way, would naturally be considered the better friends. To such a point, I think the short words of Arrian may fairly be rounded, taken as they are from immediate diaries, written on the spot at the time.[1]

In 1832, Selge had not yet been rediscovered in 'the solitary and pathless wilds of Taurus'. Nine years later both Schönborn and Daniell visited it,[2] and it has been illustrated by Langkoronski, and is now reached not often but at intervals of a few years by such travellers as have leisure to organize a small combined operation of car, jeep and horse or mule. I talked of this, and was given advice and a letter to the Müdür of the nahiye of Besh Konak, by the kind head of Antalya museum, Ismail Bey, who had been up there. Besh Konak, he said, could be reached by jeep. Jeeps were described to me as scattered about Manavgat in profusion, but there were none in Antalya and for some days nothing happened. Yet the Turk suddenly *acts*; there is an energy about him almost unnerving to anyone accustomed to the Mediterranean languor, and his activity explodes fully armed out of the most placid repose, like Athena from the head of Zeus, and as unexpected.

I had taken a room which I could leave and come back to, and this gave me the peace of mind northerners need to meet the constant unpremeditated strains; and when the taxi-driver arrived before five one morning and announced that he had heard of one of those many jeeps, I was able to pack a haversack and be ready in half an hour. The fifty-mile drive along the coast was over while the sun climbed the aqueduct of Side; and we found the (single) Manavgat jeep under a plane tree by the river, with a small morning market under way around it.

By eight-thirty we started, with bread, cucumbers, olives, sardines and beans, excellently canned locally and bought and packed beside us; and by nine o'clock we had retraced twenty-five kilometres of our morning's drive and left the main road to make across cultivation for Tashajil, a well-to-do village at the entrance to the hills.

From here we passed two hamlets only, and covered no more than thirty-four kilometres in three hours, for the road is bad in summer and for cars impossible in winter. We followed, more or less, the Eurymedon river, cutting away from it now and then across pine-covered ridges, rough and low; or crossing gravel beds and cornfields of its tributary, the Sağiri Chay, that runs along a deep cross-shaft of the range. Daniell had taken three days to climb over the ridge of Bozburun from Sillyon, led by an old man who remembered the ruins from nineteen years before: but we kept easily near the left bank of the stream,

I

and at pleasant intervals drove beside it, between clumps of myrtle rank green in spring. The river, historic in its lower reaches with Greek victories and failures, was here a smooth and strong expanse of moving water, glistening and bending like a horse's neck and sucking at the drooping boughs of trees. We lunched beside it, where planks were stacked to push in and float when the season came; and about midday opened up the fertile lands of Besh Konak—the Five Mansions—in a green basin enclosed but open, where the current flows ringleted with curling shallows, like a god.

The Müdür of the nahiye, a fair-haired and fragile young man, came from Istanbul, and this was his first post. He liked it, though the five neat whitewashed cubes put up by the government for its officials were all the social life within his reach.

"I would wish to go with you to learn," he said, when he had sent to fetch two mules and muleteers: "But I left school at sixteen, and came here; and what can one do?" He said it with the unconscious sadness that seems to weigh on young nationalists—the result perhaps of their strange patriotism, that thinks that all except what is foreign must be bad.

The anxiety to learn, however, did not take him beyond a Roman bridge near-by, where the mules were loaded up and I was mounted.

Strabo mentions these bridges in the mountainous country which abounded with precipices and ravines and kept the Selgians from being 'at any time or on any single occasion, subject to any other people'. This one joined two cliffs with one arch across the river far below, and its road, cut in the precipice, continued to show itself at intervals, in slabs of stone placed end to end for miles into the hills.

The climb took three hours. Down in the valley, we had passed occasional travellers, riding ponies with a red cloth under a carpet-saddle, or had seen camps of Yürüks in the glades; but here solitude floated up from the vertical gorges, filled with cypress or cedar as if with black spears. The silence buried the sound of its own waters, and a thin haze, spun in the blueness of air, divided one range from another, as if the heights wore haloes. The trees closed in above us and below —juniper, with soft fresh needles; and the harder aromatic cypress; maples, with their younger leaves light against the green in damp places; carob, and Judas, some sort of rhus with round leaves and feathery purple plumes, and the red boughs of the arbutus like sudden naked arms. Higher up, the oak leaves lifted into sunlight, and their trunks, and those of a tall tree like a chestnut, stood furrowed like stone among the strange hieratic stones. These ribs of rock, symmetrically ranked, descended, one felt, into the hill's foundations, and the bare rain-washed scaffolding that shows must be a part of the hidden scaffolding of earth.

Under the movement of the sun, styrax and olives spread their luxuriant branches and slim leaves. Perhaps it was not styrax, but it looked like it and I hoped it might be so, for that was the Selgian's export, used for incense and javelins; and the olive was famous round Selge, and must surely be the tree gone back here to wildness, for nowhere else have I seen it pushing among alien thickets with such ease and splendour, as if it had not forgotten how it once owned the land.

There was a human kindness about these trees; as there was in the floor of the road whose giant stones we kept on meeting, and in a cistern scooped solid through the rock at the rim of the cliff. The hands that pruned the trees, the feet that trod the causeway, brought their centuries across the empty afternoon. Even my two boys who led the mules had fallen silent, for they had never been up here before, and were not quite sure of our path that grew smaller when it left the edge of a gorge and began again to climb. At the end of two and a half hours of complete solitude we passed near a goatherd's hut, and kept away from his dogs, and heard him talking to his herd among the tree-stems out of sight: and when I lifted my eyes, I saw near-by, looking at me, motionless under an olive as if she were a part of its shadow, a girl dressed in a torn smock as grey as its stem and with eyes as green as its leaves. Seeing her astonished I rode by in silence, thinking of myths and how naturally they grow in the life that breeds them, and seem strange only to us who look at them from a more populated world.

About sunset, when we were very weary, a softening in the landscape—not terracing, but a trace of it from the past—appeared with flat spaces of meadow, and then of ploughland. The symmetrical, natural rocks encircled this place and must have made it religious long before the days of known history or the knowledge of the Greeks. Small pointed hillocks were framed in these formal borders, and, riding by them, we reached a cemetery of stones and marble fragments scattered under high oak trees and saw the village now called Zerk which once was Selge—fifteen cottages or so scattered among prostrate columns under a Roman theatre in a hollow.

It was shallow as a saucer and the ploughed fields filled it, and small pinnacles surrounded it, where temples had stood on easy slopes. Beyond them, the high peaks rose with unseen valleys intervening—Bozburun in the north-west, and Karadagh across the Eurymedon, and Ovajik smoothly edged with snow in the south-east: the names are Derme and Keriz on the map, but the people of Zerk call them by the faces that they see. Some in light and some in shadow, they had the cold pink mountain glow upon them as we made for an alpine cottage built between the marble shafts of some forgotten public building. This was the muhtar's house, under a roof weighted for snow with stones. A verandah with broad eaves held the wife's loom with the living room behind it, while the stables occupied the floor below.

A porch to sit on was built out in the open, and here we

climbed by a particularly difficult ladder, and the Müdür's letter was handed round till someone young and recently educated could be found to read it. A feeling of gloom deepened as they read. When they had all taken it in, the muhtar, tall and rough, and rather stupid, but with the dignity which even a small habit of authority gives, sat darkly fingering the note, and I began to fear either that there was a feud with the authorities—which would have been most likely in Arabia but almost unthinkable in Turkey—or else that this village was fanatically prejudiced against strangers. My muleteers were too young to explain things in the presence of their elders, and it was only after a long time, when I had been settled in the village guest-house and a fire was lighted, that I gathered from one man and another what the trouble was about.

The little place was desperately poor. The cornfields, which had looked meagre to my eyes as I rode by them, had had no snow that year—and there is no water in Zerk for irrigation except what comes from the snow: the wizened stalks were there, upright but dead. There was no food, even for a night, for our animals, and after a long discussion among the elders a youth had been sent across the hills to where the year had been a little better and enough fodder for one meal could be found. I had planned to spend a second day in Selge, but the thought filled everyone with dismay, and I there and then renounced it.

It is like an abyss opening at one's feet to look into the face of starvation, and see the earth turn barren, and know that unless it feeds us we must die. The villagers, with their sad dignity, went on with all their hospitable rites. The muhtar's wife brought a carpet for the floor, and mattresses, bolster and rugs to lay upon it; a fire (and timber was plentiful) made the hearth under its wooden canopy in the dark little room more cheerful; and a scanty dish of rice, a bowl of yaourt and water, and some flaps of bread were prepared. The muhtar and I and the muleteers ate—and then one or two of the Elders, and I took as little as I could and watched while my canned beans made a feast. No one mentioned them; no one took more than their share or tried to do so; but our metal plate was as bright as if it had been polished when the meal was over. An easier atmosphere began to creep about us; a sliver of pine thrown on at intervals kept up the firelight and the villagers dropped in one by one from their labours, and sat or squatted all together, far or near according to their station and their age. There was still hope, they said; for, though the wheat had dried, the maize was sown and rain, if it came, would save it, although the season was over; and a silence fell, as everyone thought for himself of what would happen if no rain came.

Mr. George Bean, who collects Greek inscriptions, had been up here as he has been to most places in Turkey, and had brought his sister three years before. He was remembered with friendliness, and I too was grateful to him, for not only had he made the village understand what a traveller wants to see, but he had also made it possible for me to sleep alone. When the moment came, my two young muleteers showed every intention of sharing the guest-room, now warm and comfortable with its fire; and the Elders looked perplexed when I said firmly that other quarters must be found. It was only through the example of Mr. Bean, who had left his sister in her seclusion, that the two reluctant muleteers were taken away and I was left in darkness and peace; till a man half in at the window in the middle of the night startled me by asking for his donkey. Someone, he thought, had taken it, and leaning into my torch-light like the bandit in *Rigoletto*, he looked at me in a dazed way and retreated.

Zerk and its fields were beginning to stir in the half-light when I awoke. Men, with ploughs laden on donkeys or oxen were setting out to work in the hope of rain, and the women were at the back of their cottages gathering sticks for a fire. The muhtar's wife came with a teapot across the level ploughland, and put a few sticks together, and dug a hole in the ashes, and poured me out two little glasses of tea. The Elders who had nothing to do came drifting over, and we began to walk about the ruins, beginning with the theatre and going on from pinnacle to pinnacle, in and out of the ancient walls.

In its crown of mountains the city must have been something of a miracle, through the heyday of the Greco-Roman world. Surprise, the magic of life, must always have hung about it in its remoteness, even then, when there were twenty thousand of its sons to defend it.[3] There cannot have been many travellers up and down the stone-built road from the deep valley, even when Laodice, a Pontic princess, spent her youth here, late in the 3rd century B.C., in the time of the Hellenistic kings.[4] Logbasis, a citizen of Selge, had brought her up 'tenderly loved as a daughter' in his house, and she married Achaeus, his friend, who later revolted against Antiochus III and died in Sardis.

Polybius[5] tells how the Selgians were besieging Pednelissus, which is now Baulo or Bala, a day-and-a-half's ride away (they told me), beyond Közeli in the west. These people sent to ask Achaeus for assistance, and his general came with an army and the men of Aspendus to help him; and after various feints and battles in the passes, the men of Selge were defeated. Their enemies reached the gates of the city; and Logbasis, because of his known friendship with Achaeus, was sent out to them to parley. He offered to hand over the town and a truce was granted, while Achaeus was sent for in secret and the negotiations were drawn out till he came. Then Logbasis, who had quietly hidden many of the enemy in his house, advised the citizens to call an assembly to debate on a peace. Even the sentries came down from the little hills to join in the deliberation, while Achaeus and his general, with separate forces, were marching. They were making for the Cesbedium, the acropolis temple to Zeus, and no one was there except a goatherd to see them; but he ran to warn the men of Selge, who rushed to their walls and held them, while the crowd climbed the roof of Logbasis' house and killed him and his followers and his sons.

All this can be traced plainly, though the people of Zerk and their ploughing have destroyed the city in the hollow, and the Cesbedium is flattened on its hill in ruins, and the other temples and the churches that followed them are prostrate too. They are heaped about, with hidden or weathered sculpture, and the foundations of streets of shops between them. The market floor is bare to its arched gateway; and the theatre is built into the hill with stone that crumbles, and in its crevices the bushes hang in air.

The city went on after the death of Logbasis, and made peace and signed a treaty with Achaeus in 218 B.C. It fought Pergamum, and, four centuries and a half later, in A.D. 399, was still able to withstand the attack of Tribigild the Goth, with the 'audacity which becomes temerity, and has always distinguished the Selgians in war'.[6]

It died slowly, probably of thirst, on the summits of its hills. The streams, that were brought from beneath Bozburun, where they still gather in a dip of the pine-slopes, have lost their ancient conduits; their reservoir on the acropolis is empty, and the stone brackets and the earthenware pipes that distributed them, a foot in diameter and over an inch in thickness, lie about in pieces. The cisterns under the houses have fallen in with the ruin of the houses above them; and water, the city's life, has trickled through the blind labyrinths piled up in the pillared darkness of the mountain, until far below, between the cliffs that make it useless for long stretches, the beautiful waters reappear and waste themselves at sea. Only a drip now oozes out below the southern wall of Selge, where a Nausicaa was washing in a dingy way over a cauldron, with a gourd whose lengthened shape provided a handle used for a dipper beside her.

As we climbed down a young girl met us carrying this

household water on her shoulder in a tin. She turned, as the custom is, to face the ditch away from us as we passed, and stood there, her chin and forehead wound in a white veil, knowing perhaps that her profile was beautiful against the snowy mountains. The gesture, so modest and so noble, had the grace of a ritual, leading the poor life like a quiet and certain step in a procession, over ground that has been trodden firm by many feet before.

The whole of Selge was visible from the south-eastern pinnacle. The pillars of a church aisle lay among bushes of small blossom like blackthorn on the ground, and the market and Cesbedium, the southern walls below them and the necropolis beyond curved in a semicircle round the theatre and houses of Zerk and the ruins in the hollow. The Elders who sat with me in the sun kept on asking: "Were they men made like us, who built these things?"

They would have understood more easily if I could have said that they were giants: and as I sat there I began to wonder myself, as I often do, what makes the difference and what it is.

In the middle of the 4th century B.C. the Selgians changed their barbaric coins for Greek patterns modelled on Aspendus. A hundred years later they claimed a Greek origin.[7] It was the fashion, and even before Alexander the hellenizing process had begun. Greek culture had spread on its own merits, and princes—such as Mausolus, or Abdastart, 'Slave of Astarte' at Sidon who called himself Strato—were anxious to be known by Greek names.

But chiefly Alexander altered the complexion of Asia 'so that Homer was commonly read, and the children of the Persians, of the Susianians and of the Gedrosians learned to chant the tragedies of Sophocles and Euripides'.[8] No empire before or since has been so persuasive, nor has any conversion except a religious one been so complete and widespread as was his hellenizing of the Asiatic world.

Now that the British peace is over and the world fluid, and refugees pour once again from the east,* it is no waste of time to think of these causes, that made him successful where nearly everyone else has failed. For his was no swift military triumph, that leaves a red scar and is over; nor was he a deliverer, rescuing the oppressed; nor did he come with a great army, for he had not more than about thirty thousand men when he landed, and most of the recruits made were natives of the nations he subdued. But he had, first of all, the excellence of Greek civilization which the Macedonians themselves and all the tribes they conquered believed in; and—since such superiority often spreads a religion, but rarely a political power—he had his own individual dream of the general brotherhood of man.* It came, apparently, by gradual steps, and there were signs, even in his lifetime, of its failure; and after his death the nobility and the glory departed. The vision was forgotten or merely not understood until our own day, when its future is equally obscure. Yet it led him to say things which, for two thousand years, only Saints and Prophets were aware of; and, alienating him from many of his own people, it bound him strangely to the Asiatic world.

'I took to wife a daughter of Darius,' he says to the foreign troops at Opis, 'so that I might abolish all distinction between vanquished and victor ... Asia and Europe now belong to one and the same kingdom ... It is neither unbecoming for the Persians to simulate the manners of the Macedonians, nor for the Macedonians to copy those of the Persians. Those ought to have the same rights who are to live under the same sovereign.'

'I see,' he says, 'in many nations things which we should imitate; and so great an empire cannot fitly be ruled without

* This was written during the massacre of Hungary.

contributing some things to the vanquished and learning from them. . . .'

And at last: 'If we wish to hold Asia, not merely to pass through it,' he says with a strange modernity, 'our clemency must be shared with its people.'[10]

Many steps led to this climax: the pattern of Xenophon's Cyrus, whose life he must have read before his great adventure; his direct and growing acquaintance with the peoples of Asia, begun probably with refugees at his father's court; and chiefly the natural courtesy that made him respect strangers, without which neither his nor any other brotherhood could live.

This is often recorded, in small and significant stories, such as that of his behaviour when Statira died, the wife of Darius, and 'he abstained from food and observed every honour . . . in the native manner of the Persians';[11] and the episode at Susa, where, the throne being too high and Darius' table placed as a footstool, a household eunuch wept to see his master's memory disgraced, and Alexander was for removing the table until policy and his counsellors prevailed;[12] or his meeting with Artabazus, whom he made Satrap of Bactria, and instead of walking as he usually did, ordered horses so that the old feeble man 'might not feel ashamed'.[13]

This courtesy won him the heart of Asia. It planted a seed there which has never been forgotten, and the name of the Great Alexander is familiar as no other western name in all these lands. As I looked over the crumpled Greek splendour of Selge, I wondered why it should be so hard a thing for human beings to learn; and why one must now travel chiefly in the remoter places to find it? There the traveller comes across it, as I did.

The muhtar's wife had breakfast ready when I descended. She brought honey and egg between flaps of bread to the verandah, and we sat and talked of the life of Zerk and Selge, while she fondled the last and youngest of her girls. Decked with cowry shells and talismans, and evidently loved, it tottered around, though its mother seemed unable to remember how many, exactly, she had borne. But she was definite about her seven sons.

"And when do your girls marry?" I asked.

"When their hearts are hot," she said. "That is what we are like, up here."

Matronly and gentle in her shabby slippers and long red *shirwals* or trousers, she moved about with a blue skirt wrapped below the knees, and a flowered blue quilted jacket, a red kerchief down her back hiding the hair and the circlet of coins. Her hands were fine for all their wear and toil.

She was charming, and had been beautiful, with hazel-green eyes and a regular profile, and strands of hair that were still clear red-gold under the wreath of coins and the cotton veil. In spite of all the poverty, she was serene and gay, with frank eyes that liked living; and kindness flowed like a stream about her, over the baby girl, and the smaller sons, and the cat and the guest: on a sudden impulse, putting her arms round my neck, she kissed me, and said: "Do not forget us, when you are away."

I pressed a note into her hand when the men were not about, and she hesitated for a moment, and then no doubt thought of the children and their hunger, and tied it quietly in the corner of a crimson shawl. I put a little bracelet, of the mosaics that one buys in the Square of St. Mark's, round the child's podgy wrist, and then the muhtar came up with the Elders, and we watched the mules being saddled while the men cracked walnuts for me with stones. Then I rode away sadly, as if the happiness of Zerk and its history, the olive slopes and columns and twenty thousand fighting men of Selge, and the passionate independ-ence, had died and were still dying in my sight. At the edge of the fields some boys came up with debased pieces of terra-